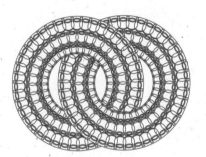

UNNATURAL SELECTION

UNNATURAL SELECTION

A Memoir

of

Adoption and Wilderness

ANDREA ROSS

CAVANKERRY
PRESS

CavanKerry Press Ltd.
Fort Lee, New Jersey
www.cavankerrypress.org

Publisher's Cataloging-In-Publication Data
(Prepared by The Donohue Group, Inc.)
Names: Ross, Andrea, 1967- author.
Title: Unnatural selection : a memoir of adoption and wilderness / Andrea Ross.
Description: First edition. | Fort Lee, New Jersey : CavanKerry Press, 2021.
Identifiers: ISBN 9781933880839 (paperback) | ISBN 9781933880846 (ePub)
Subjects: LCSH: Ross, Andrea, 1967- | Adoptees—United States—Biography. | Women park
    rangers—United States—Biography. | Families—United States. | Identity (Psychology) |
    Wilderness areas—Psychological aspects. | LCGFT: Autobiographies.
Classification: LCC HV874.82.R67 A3 2021 (print) | LCC HV874.82.R67 (ebook) |
    DDC 362.734092—dc23

Cover artwork © Adam Nixon/Stocksy United
Cover and interior text design by Ryan Scheife, Mayfly Design
First Edition 2021, Printed in the United States of America

CavanKerry Press is grateful for the support it receives from the New Jersey State Council on the Arts.

For my families: lost, found, chosen—all beloved

But nothing's lost. Or else: all is translation
And every bit of us is lost in it.

— James Merrill

Contents

Part Three: Navel of the World

Foreword

"**W**hat will my world be like now that the Earth seems to have cracked open?" is as good a question as any to ask at the edge of a journey.

Andrea Ross's book about the journey to find her birth families begins with an earthquake in California. The roof of a house ripples and heaves. A plague of acorns pummels itself to the ground. An hour away, the upper deck of San Francisco's Bay Bridge collapses.

Ross's story is all about edges, in-betweens, artifacts cut into and through stone, long views, stones that crunch beneath our sandaled feet as we walk, tectonic plates that open up holes. It's not so much a coming-of-age; it's more about what we do to make hours move from one to the next, days pass from today to tomorrow, to restart time when it has lost itself, stopped moving us ahead in life, when it is not at all clear how we convince the current to run again.

"Do you think your adoption is why you married so late?" Andrea's birth mother Elaine asks her, after they meet and begin to know each other, after Andrea describes to her, and to us, the many years she spent literally wandering the wilderness, feeling unable to move forward. When Andrea is in the depths of the Grand Canyon, drawn to its springtime warmth, we are there with her: protected by it, despite the troubles it can cause, cosseted, cocooned by its depth.

"I'd rather be outside than anywhere else," her birth father tells her the first time they speak by phone.

"I've always felt the same way," Andrea responds, bringing us with her on "the intimacy in the simple rhythms created by walking long distances with another person."

That's this astoundingly personal and public book: a long intimacy, a sleeping pad carried "to a clearing near the campfire" where we can settle in and "look up at the night sky, its vast constellations like so many blood cells pulsing through the universe, each one containing unique flaws and mysteries."

Biology makes a family. Biology doesn't make a family. The experience of being an adopted person makes both these statements true. With a poet's language of memoir, Andrea Ross searches for the phantom, the fantasy, the stories we know are there if only we can find the first stone.

"Find out if there are scholarships given by Sons of Norway. . . . Find high school yearbooks with swim team pictures. . . . Look up wedding announcements from September 1966," she is advised by a chain-smoking adoption counselor. We don't know which clue will nudge open the gate.

Along the path we see, smell, hear: dried Arizona grasses, crispy pine needles, and feathery-leaved tamarisk trees; side canyons, ledges, and alcoves; cottonwood branches and agave leaves. We journey with a veritable chorus of poets—Charles Simic, Adrienne Rich, Amy Lowell, Audre Lorde, Robert Hass, Gary Snyder, Edmund Spenser—headed toward the edge where, in the words of Chana Bloch, we "bring back something / from the brink of nothing."

It's a life we can identify with. After all, everyone has family secrets, truths we squint at through obfuscated hints, things we didn't know, didn't understand, didn't trust, maybe didn't quite want to investigate. Perhaps not all are of the order of finding birth parents and navigating the closed legality of a "sealed" birth certificate, but the finding of hidden stories is the work of becoming humanly whole.

Aren't we each just searching for our version of what Andrea Ross calls our "colony of deep belonging"?

Miriam Peskowitz,
New York Times bestselling author
of *The Daring Book for Girls*

This is primarily a work of nonfiction. Some names and characteristics have been changed, some events have been compressed or presented out of sequence, and some dialogue has been recreated. Since this is a memoir in part about closed adoption, there is certain information I do not have access to. The chapter titled "Slapped" is a fiction attempting to recreate a key scene for which I was not present. It is based on information I believe to be true from multiple sources.

Part One

Outer Space

Chapter 1

Earthquake

(Loma Mar, California)

All the new thinking is about loss.
In this it resembles all the old thinking.

—Robert Hass

A dusty scratching noise arose from the wooden planks beneath my feet. It was as if the woodrats who usually scrabbled around in the ceiling of the old staff house had suddenly shifted to a subterranean position and were desperate to escape. Then the floor began to move, undulating as the racket continued.

I struggled to stand up, guitar strapped across my chest. I had been in a few earthquakes before, but none of them had made a deafening sound like Friday night at the racetrack. I looked down at my feet, shod as usual in hiking boots. The floor rocked so violently, I was having trouble standing. The wood-paneled walls shuddered, the roof started creaking, and gritty brown ash—a century's worth of dust and woodrat shit—showered on me from between ceiling planks. I tried to brush it from my hair, but before I could remove much, the taxidermied great horned owl we used for demonstrating night vision and silent flight took a dive from its perch and thudded, puffing apart on the floor and making me jump back with a start.

I ran outside, guitar bouncing in front of me on its strap. Once clear of the house, I turned toward it. The roofline rippled and heaved like a break-dancer I'd recently watched on the streets in San Francisco's Mission District. I turned away so I wouldn't have to see it fall. Instead, I watched a grove of mature live oak trees swaying cartoonishly, like punching bags being struck repeatedly by some giant fist. Acorns thundered down on me, pelting my scalp. I covered my head, but they bruised my knuckles and banged the guitar, whose strings twanged like the soundtrack of a bad horror movie. Again I ran, looking for protection. As I neared some metal picnic tables, the racket grew even louder—the din of the acorns striking them was deafening. I crawled under a table even though I was sure a tree would fall on it and crush me. The noise and the violent earth-shaking continued, so I closed my eyes and covered my face with my hands, not wanting to see the destruction about to rip loose from the crust of the Earth: roots rising up like twisted hands, trunks crashing down. Things that don't usually move at all stirred with a crunch and a crackle.

This can't happen now, I thought. *I never got the chance to meet my birth parents.*

The roaring surge agitated around me. I curled into an even smaller ball beneath the picnic table.

And then it stopped.

I looked around. The trees were still standing, the house still intact. People emerged from various buildings and stood outside, frightened and confused looks on their faces.

It was my second day as a teacher of sixth grade environmental science at a week-long outdoor program near the Santa Cruz Mountains. My first job after college. I hadn't been trained in what to do if the biggest earthquake in eighty years occurred while I was playing guitar on my afternoon break.

"The kids are on the field!" someone yelled. We all ran out to where our students had been writing in their science journals with their classroom teachers.

The kids cried and whimpered, huddling around their teachers. Sara, the principal, ran up with a roster of everyone in residence at the school that week, and we did a headcount. All staff and students were accounted for.

————————————

Darkness would fall soon, so we led group activities on the playing field while the maintenance staff checked all the kids' cabins to see if they were safe to occupy for the night. We played silly, nobody-loses games of Blob Tag, Elbow Tag, and Everybody's It, running around in the grass and pretending everything was okay. We didn't know the extent of the damage yet, didn't know that the Marina District in San Francisco was aflame, that people had been buried alive in Santa Cruz, that the San Francisco Bay Bridge's upper deck had collapsed. But soon, the waves of bad news began to roll in via radio and telephone.

Teacher Joe decided we should do a Barn Boogie in the field while the building inspections continued. While he called the Patty-Cake Polka and the Virginia Reel, I heard from Sara that one cabin had fallen off its foundations and water spouted from the ground beneath. The electricity was out, so the square dance music came from a big silver boom box whose batteries were slowly but surely running out of power.

I ran back to the trailer that served as my bedroom to grab a sweater for the long evening ahead. I was sure I would find my boxy home rocked off its dubious foundation into the redwood forest behind it, but somehow the trailer hadn't overturned in the quake.

Inside, though, my clothing, books, and teaching supplies lay strewn across the floor as if ransacked by thieves. Bug collection boxes, hand lenses, and diagrams of the redwood tree life cycle littered the floor. I noticed my heavy, hardbound poetry anthologies piled on my bed and imagined what would have happened to me had I been there during the quake. I decided to deal with the mess later, found a sweater, and headed for the camp's office, where the only phone was located.

I wanted to try to call my parents, who lived a few hours' drive north, in Chico. I figured they were well out of the earthquake's range but would be worried about me. I also hoped to check in with my brothers. Brian, twenty-one, lived far away in Minneapolis, so I knew he was safe, and my youngest brother, Jason, was in his second year of college in southern California. I just wanted to talk to them, to let everyone know I was okay.

I heard Sara on the phone. "The school board told us to keep the kids here."

I peeked through the office's mullioned windows and saw her twiddling a pencil in the air nervously. The pencil looked rubbery, undulating in space.

"I understand, but do you really want your child to be on a bridge right now?" she asked.

I sat on the stone planter in front of the office and grabbed a stick to dig in the dirt while I waited for her call to end. I had always spent a lot of time rooting around like that. In elementary school, I hadn't liked playing sports at recess, so I dug. One day, on the baseball field near the chain-link backstop, my friend Amy and I discovered a tiny constellation of glass shards embedded in the dried hardpan soil where the grass had been worn away by kids' sneakers. Each piece of glass formed a tiny dome under which miniscule weeds had grown. Every little terrarium was a world within a world. I ran out to the baseball diamond during recess every day to polish the tiny vitrines and narrate adventures inside the fantasy worlds I imagined beneath the glass. I saw multitudes in those domes, other places in which I might live.

Sitting on that planter in front of Sara's office, I was still seeking something, looking to nature for answers. And now it was my job to take care of groups of kids away from their parents for a week at a time. Every Monday morning, busloads of sixth graders arrived in a cloud of diesel fumes at our little camp beneath the redwood trees, and it was my job to guide them through "The Nature," as many of them called it, until Friday afternoon, when they would be transported back to their parents. In the interim, I was their mother and father, their older sister and confidant, their teacher and guide. Of course, I felt unequipped. I was twenty-two years old and didn't know much about taking care of anyone. I barely knew how to take care of myself.

As I dug with the stick, I wondered, *What will my world be like now that the Earth seems to have cracked open?*

A few days later, after all the kids at the outdoor school were safely delivered home to their parents, I met Don. He had been living in a dank trailer in the redwood forest for a year when I arrived. He worked at the environmental school across the creek from mine. He had tangled brown hair, a bushy beard, and a long skinny body with huge forearms, overmuscled from rock climbing.

He wooed me by giving me watercolor paintings he'd made of snakes and fording the dark creek late at night to visit me in my little trailer, bearing chocolate and his guitar. Our first real date was on a cold Saturday night in January. He stepped into my trailer just after dusk.

"Find a winter hat and gloves," he said, his snaggletoothed smile melting me. "We're going for a night hike."

"Where to?" I asked, suiting up in warm clothes.

"It's a secret. A surprise."

When I finished bundling up, he grabbed my hand and we trotted into the dark forest. I pulled my headlamp from my pocket and put it on.

"You don't need that," Don said. "The full moon is about to rise over the ridge."

I removed the headlamp and jammed it in his jacket pocket, pulled him close to kiss him.

We trekked along by moonlight for about an hour, Don leading the way uphill, across a ridge, stopping at an especially huge redwood tree. I marveled at its backlit form.

"I call her Wanda," he said. "Because you gotta *Wanda* how old she is!"

I looked up at the tree, shaking my head at his corny pun. The tree was enormous, perhaps a thousand years old, and it had a large, burned-out section in its base that created a cavern large enough for both of us to fit inside. I climbed in with him.

"Wow," I whispered.

"This isn't the surprise—it's up there." He pointed above us and grabbed a hidden rope ladder. We climbed it twenty feet up to the tree's lowest branches, then made our way up, limb by limb. Eventually we reached a small platform built among the upper branches.

"How'd you do it?" I asked, stepping tentatively onto the platform, legs shaking with fatigue and fear of heights.

"Lars did it—he's been carrying scrap lumber up here piece by piece for weeks." Lars was another naturalist friend, a big, burly guy who probably had plans to do his own wooing up there. Don pointed to another rope dangling a few feet away. "There's the pulley system he rigged to haul it up," he said, hopping onto the platform with me.

"It's amazing," I said, looking out at the valley shimmering below us.

We sat down and carefully lowered our backs to the platform to watch the moon quiver through the damp night air, huddling against each other, foggy breath wisping from our mouths.

I *Wanda'd* if I was falling in love.

————————————

The school year wore on, the earthquake damage to the camp buildings was slowly repaired, and Don introduced me to more new things. One day he drove me to a used wilderness equipment store in Berkeley and bought a pair of climbing shoes with gummy black leather soles. He handed them to me with a big smile, and I was a little stunned—I'd never had a boyfriend before who bought me such gifts.

From there, we drove directly to Split Rock, a small climbing area in a Marin County open space preserve with a gorgeous view of the San Francisco Bay and the luscious green hills of spring.

Don scrambled up the rock and set up a top rope anchor so he could teach me to climb. I sat at the bottom of the crag, loosening the laces on my new climbing shoes so I could jam my feet into them. The shoes were tight and uncomfortable. My heart raced. I grew more nervous by the second, to the point that I had trouble tying the laces.

I didn't really understand how rock climbing worked—what was the rope for, anyway? And why would I want to climb up the face of something that I could easily walk up the back of? But I cinched up the shoes and stood. I wanted to be a badass. I wanted to like climbing. I wanted to be a cool climber-girl, windswept and rugged-looking like the ones I'd watched dancing up stone at Indian Rock in Berkeley.

Don finished setting the anchor and scrambled down the rock. He helped me buckle into his spare climbing harness, showing me how to make sure to double back the waist belt. "It won't hold in a fall unless you do that," he said. "When you're climbing, you have to be very careful to check everything and check it again or it could be deadly."

I didn't like the sound of that at all. What if the equipment failed? I preferred low-tech, grounded activities. Hiking suited me; to hike I needed nothing but my own muscles and a pair of shoes.

Don threaded his climbing rope through two parts of my harness. "We're going to tie you in now. This knot is called a figure eight on a bight. It will hold you if you fall, and you can untie it even after it's been weighted." He showed me how to tie it, then undid it. He handed it to me. "Now you try."

I coiled the rope into an "8" shape.

"Is this right?" I asked. My hands visibly shook, but I tried to ignore them. Climbing was Don's passion. And I wanted to be Don's passion too.

"That's right," he said. He tugged on the knot to make sure it was tight, then slipped his arms around my waist and pulled me to him. "Let's get you on the rock!"

I gave him the most confident smile I could muster—probably not very convincing. He put me on belay, threading the rope through a device in his harness that would keep me from falling if I lost my balance. He stood on the ground watching me and keeping taut the rope connecting us as I worked my way up the face of the crag to climb.

I didn't die. I didn't even fall. I also didn't love it. All that airiness terrified me.

And ever since the earthquake, I had thought about finding my birth parents. I hadn't died in the quake, but who knew what could happen? Especially if I continued rock climbing.

Chapter 2

Inflamed

(Santa Cruz, California)

The truth does not change according to our ability to stomach it.

—Flannery O'Connor

I was born in Denver in 1967, placed in foster care when I was one day old, and adopted by another family three weeks later. In those days, "closed" adoptions were the norm. In closed adoption, the birth parents and the adoptive parents agree to anonymity, and they sign away their rights to know who the other party is. The idea was that this arrangement would allow birth mothers to move on with their lives, leaving behind what was thought of as the tragedy of unwed pregnancy. It also allowed adoptive parents to pretend there was no other mother, no other family to whom their baby belonged, and it ensured that no birth parents would come knocking on doors, demanding their baby back.

My closed adoption was one pretense after another: in accordance with state laws, my original birth certificate was "sealed," and an amended one issued. This new birth certificate declared that I had been born at "Hospital" and delivered by "Doctor," further encrypting my origins. The name of the woman who had given birth to me was removed from the document, and the names of my adoptive parents were inserted in her place.

I first read this document as a young teen, when I applied for a passport to travel with my family. It made me feel anonymous to read this false birth certificate, as if I hadn't been born at all.

As soon as I could understand it, my parents told me I was adopted. At first, because of how they normalized it, I didn't give it much thought. But as a preadolescent, I began imagining who my birth parents might be.

Someone had once told me I looked like Natalie Wood. At the time, I didn't know anything about her except that she was a movie star, but I liked the idea of being a movie star's long-lost daughter. I watched *West Side Story*. I found a picture of Natalie Wood with long dark hair and almond shaped eyes, wearing a black crepe nineteen-sixties cocktail dress. That photograph decided it for me: she was definitely my birth mother. I had a celebrity birth mom, and no one knew but me.

Toward the end of my second year of college, I awoke one day in my futon on the floor of my student apartment, and every joint in my body hurt. I didn't have enough energy to get out of bed and eat a bowl of cereal, much less attend my classes that day. The next day was the same. So was the following one.

After a few weeks of achy listlessness, doctor visits, and blood draws, I finally saw a rheumatologist who concluded I had some kind of inflammatory disease similar to lupus or rheumatoid arthritis, but not diagnosable as either one. The doctor prescribed anti-inflammatory medication for me and ordered more bloodwork.

I looked up lupus in a medical journal at the university library, and learned that it's an incurable autoimmune disorder that can cause heart problems, kidney failure, and stroke. In a literature class I had learned that Flannery O'Connor had died from lupus at the age of thirty-nine, leaving stories unwritten, a life half-lived. I felt alone and scared, wondering about my own fate.

My parents were readying to leave on a trip to England, so they weren't able to visit me or take care of me. I was hurt that they had chosen to depart on the trip rather than help me, even though I knew it was unreasonable. It was a transatlantic trip, after all. Yet I was their child, wasn't I? And I had a mysterious disease that might kill me.

One morning during the third week of being sick, I was woken up by an unbearable itchy feeling all over my body. When I pried my eyes open to look at myself, I saw hives all over my arms, legs, torso. I began to cry, loudly. My roommate Jen heard me wailing and stuck her head into my room.

"You okay?"

"Look at me!" I said, sitting up in bed, still sobbing. "Now something else is happening!" I extended my red spotted arms to show her. "It just keeps getting worse! I'm afraid I'm dying!"

Jen sat down on the edge of my futon and put her hand on my shoulder.

I cried even harder. "I don't know what to do! I feel like shit, I'm in so much pain, and now there are itchy bumps all over my body! I don't know what's happening!" I rolled over onto my side, curling into a fetal position.

"It's going to be okay," she said, rubbing my back. "I'll call your rheumatologist."

"But it's eight o'clock on Saturday morning!" I wailed. "No one will be there."

"I'll get ahold of her," Jen said. "Where's her number?"

I was dumbstruck. My nineteen-year-old roommate was taking control in a way that I wished I could, wished my parents would. I shambled over to my desk and riffled through scraps of paper.

"Here it is." I handed the number to her. Walking to my desk had made my knees hurt. I looked down at my legs. Like my arms, they too were covered with bright red hives. I sank into my desk chair and began to cry again.

Jen gently reached over and wrapped a blanket around my shoulders. "It's going to be okay. We're going to figure this out. Just sit tight for a minute while I call the doctor, alright?"

I nodded tearily, and she walked into the living room to call. Through the wall, I could hear her talking on the phone, which made me cry harder, this time with relief. I was miserable, I wanted someone to take care of me, and Jen was doing just that.

A few minutes later, she came back into my bedroom. I was scratching at the hives on my legs.

"I talked to your doctor, and she said she would meet you at her office in an hour."

I stopped scratching and looked up at her.

"Really?" I couldn't believe it. I had never made an emergency call to a doctor before, had never asserted myself like that. *You can just do that?* I thought. I had always accepted whatever hand was dealt to me, no questions asked. I had never felt I had a right to complain. "Thanks," I said, feeling a little better.

"You're welcome. Now let's go make some breakfast."

I followed her into the kitchen, running my palms across my bumpy arms, trying not to rub at them. They were on fire with itch.

An hour later I saw the doctor, who diagnosed the rash as an allergic reaction to the anti-inflammatory medication she'd prescribed a few days before.

"Just stop taking it and the rash will go away. In the meantime, you can use some Benadryl cream. You'll be fine," she said.

I was relieved the rash would subside, but I didn't believe I would be fine. I was scared I was going to die from whatever malady had taken root in my body.

My twentieth birthday came a few days later. I was still exhausted and mown down. The rheumatologist had explained that my fatigue was due to anemia, which was caused by inflammatory cells in my bloodstream.

I stayed in bed most of my birthday, banking what little energy I had because Jen's mother had offered to take us to a Thai restaurant for my birthday dinner. As evening drew near, I crawled out of bed, donned a wrinkled dress, applied anti-itch cream to my splotchy limbs, and dragged a comb through the mat of hair at the back of my head that had been entangling itself as I lay in bed hour after hour.

I ushered in my twenties exhausted, covered in hives, eating pad Thai with my roommate and her mother. I was far from home, overwhelmed with fear, and looking for comfort. Spicy noodles would have to suffice.

The rash eventually faded, but my pain and fatigue did not abate. My lab results confirmed systemic inflammation, indicating some sort of autoimmune disorder. For the first time in my life, I realized I needed to find out something about my biological parents: I needed to obtain their medical history to see if there were any clues to what was wrong with me. But to get that information, I needed their names, and their names were on my original birth certificate, sealed away.

Chapter 3

Non-Identified

(Santa Cruz and Los Altos Hills, California)

I'm Nobody! Who are you?
Are you – Nobody – Too?

—Emily Dickinson

During my high school summers, I had been an assistant counselor at a Girl Scout camp although at the time I hadn't really been interested in the "camping" part of the job; instead, I wanted independence from my parents and relief from the hot boredom of summer in my hometown. I wanted a paycheck and a challenge. At the Girl Scout camp, I found those things and more.

Everyone on staff was female—there were no boys to flirt with, so my psyche was freed up to do other things. I wrote and directed plays for my group of campers, called "Meadow Murfs," made up songs and skits and performed them at nightly campfires, and learned to live in a little two-person canvas tent for three months.

Per Girl Scout tradition, each counselor had to give herself a camp nickname. I shared a tent with the head counselor, a college student who had nicknamed herself "Lifer" because, as she explained, she loved life. I was skeptical of her sunny optimism. I had nicknamed myself "Bug," which speaks volumes about how I felt about myself.

Lifer was the real deal—she really did love life. Plus, she was smart, kind, and funny. I found myself wanting to be like her. She had long blond hair and squinty eyes from smiling and being outside. She didn't seem to care much about what she looked like or how she dressed, but she radiated beauty and confidence and compassion. She was far beyond all the high school pettiness and self-consciousness that I was embroiled in. Yet she treated me as an equal, and I was grateful to have the opportunity to be myself without fear of ridicule that summer. I liked our little canvas platform tent with old army cots in it—it was like having my own house for the first time. But Lifer slept outside the tent every night.

"I love having no walls between me and the wilderness," she told me when I asked her why she didn't sleep in the tent. I didn't understand. But the more I hung out with Lifer, the more I learned to love living outdoors.

Four years later, I found myself wanting to duck back into that lifestyle. I was now about the age that Lifer had been when I met her. Could I become more like her by working at a camp again? Could I rekindle in myself that sense of equanimity and joy of belonging in my environs that I had experienced when I was with her?

A month before I got sick, I had attended a summer job fair on campus and interviewed for a position as a counselor at a farm and wilderness camp.

During the interview with the camp's director, I tried channeling Lifer's confidence and competence. And even though I had never backpacked before, I got a job guiding backpack trips for teenagers through the trails of California's Coast Range.

I signed the contract before I got sick. As my semester ended, I began to wonder whether I could do the job. But I wanted to ignore my symptoms, fatigue, and aching joints and go out into the coastal mountains and prove myself. I didn't want to admit that I probably wasn't physically up to the task.

A few weeks before our lease ended, I began packing my things into storage before showing up at the summer camp for work. Something about living among the chaos of all my belongings scattered in and around boxes all over my room gave me an extra push to try to cultivate some internal organization in my life.

I threaded the telephone cord out my bedroom window and climbed onto the patio in our tiny yard. I grabbed a mildewed patio chair and sat down as the city bus rolled by, shaking the ground beneath me like an earthquake.

Nestled among the calla lilies that grew in the yard, I took a deep breath and dialed the number for Lutheran Social Services in Denver. A social worker named Danielle answered the phone. I explained my health crisis to her and asked her to look through my records for any health history of inflammation, arthritis, or worse. She said she'd send me what she could.

A week later, I received in the mail a short excerpt from the agency's records, which revealed only that my maternal grandmother had suffered from varicose veins. I called Danielle back. Upon further probing, she explained that there was very little medical information in my file. She also told me about something called non-identifying information.

"There's a document that we can release to you if you request it. It contains information about the circumstances surrounding your birth, minus any identifying names and details," she said.

I squirmed. "You have more information about my birth mother?"

"Yes," Danielle said. "The document would be excerpted from the information she gave us when she placed you for adoption."

At that moment, I was much more concerned with finding the cause of the pain in my body than the circumstances surrounding my birth. I didn't think I needed any non-medical information, so I thanked her and ended the phone call.

Instead of pursuing my genes, I attempted to exorcise whatever evil thing had taken residence in my joints by trying to outpace it. I bought a mountain bike and planned to try pedaling up the hilly trails near the summer camp. I figured over time, surrounded by coast redwood trees, I would grow a little stronger.

When I arrived at camp, I didn't tell anyone I was sick. I didn't ask for a lighter assignment. I didn't say anything at all. I just showed up to counselor training with one of those soft, pack cloth suitcases that converts to a backpack, several kinds of anti-inflammatory medications, some cheap hiking boots I'd bought at a sporting goods store, and my secret illness. I felt anxious about my disability, guilty for not disclosing it, and worried about my rookie status as a backpacker.

The rheumatologist had diagnosed me with some sort of inflammatory arthritis, but it was still inconclusive. And there I was at camp, hoping to regain some vestigial sense of self that had drained away since I had gotten sick.

The camp was located in the dry, sunny foothills of the Santa Cruz Mountains. Our group base-camped in a grove of madrones and oaks, where we taught campers how to make tea from curls of cinnamon-colored madrone bark and pillows filled with mugwort leaves.

We led them on trips along the ridgelines of Big Basin State Park and through the redwoods. Trekking was a struggle since I was still anemic. And thinking was difficult too—I was so fatigued. During our first backpacking trip, as I hiked along with my silly suitcase-backpack strapped to my body, enormous blisters formed on each of my big toes. When I removed my boots, the blisters protruded like little balloons—painful ones. I tried layering moleskin around them to pad them, to no avail. The first day back in camp, both of my humongous blisters popped. I led the subsequent backcountry trip with raw toes. New blisters formed in the same places. Desperate, I borrowed someone's Swiss Army knife and cut two round holes on the sides of my cheap boots. My toes felt better, but my feet looked ridiculous, like a hobo's.

The upside was, I didn't have a lot of energy to be embarrassed about my rookie mistakes. The intermittent fog of the coastal mountains we hiked through mirrored my own mental state.

At first, it was all I could do to get through the long days of camp counseling. But over the course of the summer, with the help of cortisone pills the rheumatologist had prescribed, the pain subsided to a tolerable level, and I regained some of my energy.

Coastal California summers are virtually rain-free, so we slept outside every night. During the periods between treks, when our group stayed at our little base camp in the grove, I carried my sleeping pad to a clearing near the campfire and settled in to look up at the night sky, its vast constellations like so many blood cells pulsing through the universe, each one containing unique flaws and mysteries.

One night, I held up my left thumb and inspected it in the moonlight. As a child, I had sucked it, envisioning myself as a baby, curled fetally and floating in outer space amid twinkling stars, with my umbilicus threading out from my belly, connected to nothing. I wondered who my real belly button had been connected to. I believed my thumb enabled me to communicate with the aliens I had probably come from, thumb-sucking a direct phone line connecting me to the universe, and to whoever might be looking for me out there and wanting to bring me back to the mothership.

I could not understand why anyone would want to keep me from doing it, but when I entered kindergarten, my parents and teachers told me to stop. No one gave me a good reason. They didn't know what they were missing, how great it was. The adults in my life became increasingly fervent in their insistence that I cease and desist, so my thumb and I had to go underground. I did whatever I could to hide my habit, but I had no intention of stopping.

Teachers wrote, "Thumb Sucker" in scarlet letters on my report cards, and I felt ashamed, but not ashamed enough to stop. The way I saw it, there were no negative consequences except scorn from adults.

One night, when I was about eight, I was lying in bed, sucking my thumb, reading a book. My mom had told me to clean my room, but I hadn't done it. She walked into my room and found me sucking my thumb, surrounded by a mess.

"You have *got* to *stop that!*" she yelled, picking up a shoe from the floor and throwing it at me. I ducked away from the shoe flying at my head, chin trembling and cheeks burning. By then, my mom was gone. She had slammed the door and stomped off. I was mystified by how furious my thumb-sucking made her. She often seemed overwhelmed by the job of parenting three young children. I spent a lot of time trying to stay out of her way. But she was rarely violent like this; usually she was just angry or sad. Why was she so opposed to me sucking my thumb? Perhaps on some level, she knew it was a kind of soothing she couldn't provide. Perhaps she was frustrated with not being able to solve the problem. But why were other adults opposed to my thumb-sucking? It wasn't hurting anyone. On the contrary, it made my life better. Much better.

What finally turned the thumb-sucking tide? When I was ten, an orthodontist told me, "If you don't stop sucking your thumb, your teeth will never be straight."

Maybe I was ready to accept the responsibility of being a member of the outer world and to let go of that part of my inner world. Or maybe it was just that the orthodontist had finally offered the logical reason I needed to change my behavior. I stopped cold turkey, never returning to it.

Lying under the stars at the wilderness camp, I wished I still sucked my thumb. Or at least that I could regain that feeling of connection with the universe. I was an alien with no way to make contact, a little adopted girl who felt disconnected and didn't know why.

———

The next day, I sent a letter to the adoption agency, requesting my non-identifying information.

When the document arrived in the mail, I drove to a café in town that had thick coffee and wait staff who never bothered me no matter how long I sat there. My stomach churned as I clutched three typewritten pages describing my biological parents' ages, weights, heights, and hobbies at the time of my birth, as well as descriptions of their immediate family members.

I spread the pages before me on a wobbly table. Seeing my genetic and cultural heritage condensed to three sparse pages of text made my stomach drop (was that all there was to me?) and my insides feel like they were vibrating (I had origins!). I finally had details I could use to fill in my mental picture of Natalie Wood, my fantasy birth mother. According to the document, my birth mother was eighteen years old, and five feet seven inches tall. She had hazel eyes and a complexion that tanned easily, was of Norwegian extraction on both sides of her family, and was an only child. I blinked rapidly. I had never guessed that I was half Norwegian. People had told me I looked French, Native American—any number of things. Others told me I looked just like my adoptive mom and dad, who were Finnish and Scottish, respectively. I had never considered I might be Norwegian. What did it mean? Was I a Viking? I chuckled, imagining it.

I learned that my birth mother got allergies from pollen in the springtime, and liked to play the piano. The notes said she was always a "B" student who liked to write poetry in her leisure time and was on a swim team in high school. She had completed two quarters of college before "needing to make plans related to her pregnancy." I thought about my adoptive mom, a brainy college professor several years older than my birth mom.

The notes also mentioned that my birth parents met through friends and attended the same college. They dated steadily for a while before she became pregnant, and it was upsetting to her when she learned that my birth father married another woman, who was also pregnant, eight months before I was born.

I stopped reading, stomach wobbling from this unexpected turn (and too much coffee). I'd never guessed I might have a half-sibling almost the same age as me. *What kind of a man would get two girls pregnant at the same time?* I wondered, a lump in my throat forming as I thought about my birth mother as the not-chosen girl. Now I knew we were both not-chosen girls. I felt a new affinity to her. And I finally had a few pieces of the puzzle of my history. It was like a game of Clue, a mystery to solve.

The notes said my birth father was aware of my birth mother's pregnancy and admitted paternity, but her parents did not want him involved with her or the pregnancy in any way.

I felt even sicker to my stomach. *What had happened? Were they cruel? Angry? Overwhelmed?*

I read on: when I was born, my birth father was twenty-two years old. He was described as a good-looking young man with light brown wavy hair and brown eyes who was large-boned and athletic, playing football in high school. He quit college when he got married to the other pregnant girl, and began working with his father in an irrigation supply business to support his new family. My birth father had left to live another life without my birth mother or me. My ribs tightened, breath quickened.

The café staff had begun wiping down the tables around me, getting ready to close up for the night. I gathered my papers, now slightly greasy from pieces of old croissants on the table, and slumped into the evening.

As I walked to my car, I realized that despite the initial thrill of reading that document, and the shocking news I had a half-sibling somewhere who was almost a twin, I still knew nothing about the inflammatory arthritis I seemed to have developed, or of any other genetic disease. Also, the information seemed whitewashed: what middle-class, Caucasian teenage girl in the 1960s didn't play piano? What red-blooded American boy didn't play football?

It was difficult to imagine those faces, personalities, or home lives. They seemed like caricatures, drawn with quick, broad strokes. The adoption agency had done its job well: this was truly "non-identifying information." I wondered if the social workers had fabricated these "facts," or at least changed some of the details from the original records they held to shroud the truth.

Nonetheless, it was the first information I had received about my biological origins, and during the course of the summer, I read the pages over and over, looking for snippets of familiarity: I had sandy blond hair and greenish-brown eyes, I liked playing piano, I liked writing poetry, loved singing. Perhaps I had gotten those attributes from them. But did they love the outdoors? Were they kind? Were they alive?

Back at camp, the summer wound down. My illness had left me so fatigued, I had little spare energy to be fun for my campers, and nothing left to give to my fellow counselors. I had made it through the season as a backpacking guide, but just barely, trudging through the summer carrying my suitcase-backpack, learning wilderness skills on the fly. I knew I hadn't really pulled my weight. I was not the backpacking guide I had pictured myself becoming before I got sick.

After saying good-bye, I drove back to school through late summer shadows, accompanied by the documents from the adoption agency, which had stoked a tiny ember of determination. I was ready to tackle my final two years of college—and to spend them with a new kind of mindfulness: of my body and my desire to belong.

Chapter 4

Slapped

(Northern Colorado)

what first felt like an insult to the flesh
Was the blank "o" of love.

—Larry Levis

This is how I imagine it:

It's January in northern Colorado. A snowstorm begins to blow across the Front Range, across the fallow fields and cattle farms surrounding the college. Just outside her cinderblock dormitory on the edge of campus, my birth mother Elaine, a first-year college student, lugs her hamper to the next dorm to do laundry.

Olive, her ex-boyfriend's mother, gray-haired, strong, appears unexpectedly, walking in from the parking lot. She blocks Elaine's path. "Say you're not pregnant!" she snaps.

Elaine stops, unable to say or do anything. Both women stand in the cold, quivering with rage, fear, staring at each other for a long moment.

Olive growls again, "Say you're not pregnant!"

Elaine, still paralyzed with shock and fear, holds the laundry basket tight against her belly. Olive reaches out and slaps Elaine across her cheek, and Elaine drops the basket. A few socks tumble to the pavement, limp birds downed in a storm. Snow flurries swirl in the air, settle on the fallen laundry. Now visible, Elaine's belly protrudes tellingly.

Elaine's dorm-mate pokes her head out of a second-story window to see what's going on, and my birth mother quietly says to Olive, "I'm not pregnant."

Olive replies in a low voice, "That's right. You stay away from my son! He's married now!" She turns briskly and hurries back to her car. Elaine stands in the cold, one hand on her belly.

––––––––––

Elaine's father, John, walks in the front door of his white clapboard house, carrying a letter he has just opened. He waves it toward his wife. "Did you know about this?" he asks. He is yelling. His face is red.

Teresa was standing at the sink washing dishes. "What in heaven's name is going on?" She wipes her hands on her apron and takes the letter from her husband's outstretched hand, reads it. She gasps and lowers herself onto the vinyl upholstery of the nearest kitchen chair.

John has an idea that whatever is going on has something to do with the boy Elaine has dated on and off for the past year.

Alarmed, they try to call Elaine, but the dorm phone's rings echo like a song down the hallway. No one answers. Elaine's parents decide they must go find her, and they rush to their silver Chevy, her mother still clasping the college's letter in her hand. They drive the forty miles north, from Longmont to Greeley, to find out why their daughter has quit school. Even in winter, the smell from the cattle feedlots makes its way into the car.

Soon, Elaine's parents are knocking at her dormitory door. They mean to interrogate her with a barrage of questions, but the instant she opens the door they see the small, gravid bump straining at her blue dress. They have their answer.

Elaine's eyes tear up when she sees them.

John and Teresa step inside Elaine's small bedroom and close the door behind them. In a gravelly voice, John says, "Who's the father?"

Elaine stares at the floor, holding back sobs.

"You've ruined your life! You've ruined our lives!" her mother says, panic on her face. She turns to her husband. "What are we going to do?" She folds her arms across her body as if a draft has blown into the room.

"Does Theo know?" John demands. His left hand grips the letter, now crumpled, a spent peony.

Elaine nods. She knows her parents know that Theo has married another pregnant girl. They know she herself attended their wedding. This unspoken fact hangs thickly in the air: there will be no shotgun wedding for Elaine. The other girl's father has seen to that.

Elaine begins to cry openly and sits down on her narrow bed. Her father continues to stand, his face reddening again. He says nothing.

"What were you thinking, Elaine? That you could quit school and have a baby in this dorm room without us knowing?" asks her mother, sinking down on the bed next to Elaine. In a softer voice, she says, "Why didn't you tell us?"

John opens the closet door, riffles around for a suitcase, and places one on the bed next to her. "Pack your things. We're leaving."

Elaine and her parents pack her belongings quickly, a plush toy puppy from the bed, her college-girl clothing. At one point when her parents aren't looking, Elaine slides a photograph between the pages of her diary.

It's of herself and Theo dressed up for her high school prom: she wears long pink evening gloves and a burgundy velvet gown, her hair is arranged in a spun-sugar bouffant topped with a little white bow, and her eyes sparkle mischievously as she gazes up at his goofy, smiling face. She doesn't want her parents to destroy this picture, snapped not quite a year before.

The three of them drive in silence back to their house in Longmont, arriving in time to eat a late supper at home. After washing the dishes, Elaine retreats to her bedroom. It feels cozy, familiar. She begins to relax. Maybe everything will be all right, she thinks: she is home with her parents, away from school where her friends were wondering why she wasn't attending classes. She has her bedroom, her stuffed animals covering the bed. She imagines living there throughout the pregnancy. Maybe her mother will help with the baby. Maybe she hasn't ruined their lives.

She hasn't told them that Theo's mother slapped her. She won't.

———————

The next morning at the breakfast table, John announces that Elaine will not be staying with them at home, nor will she keep the baby. He has already called the Florence Crittenden Home for Unwed Mothers in Denver, arranging for Elaine to stay there until the baby is born.

"We expected better from you," he says.

"I'm so sorry, Dad." She stares at a plate of scrambled eggs her mother has set in front of her. She is ravenous, hungry all the time now, but she cannot pick up her fork. Her father's disgust has immobilized her.

"You need to put this behind you so you can live a normal life. Do you understand me?"

"Yes," she says softly.

"It'll be like it never happened," Teresa says, standing near Elaine's seated form, tentatively stroking Elaine's long brown hair. She glances at her husband, then back at Elaine.

"Later you'll be able to marry a good man and have children with him when it's the right time."

"But it—" Elaine stops herself. She gazes at her belly straining against the shift she found in her closet. She knows better than to suggest that now could be the right time to have a baby. Her father is a fierce man with a temper and no patience for what he calls "nonsense." Elaine's feelings about this matter qualify as nonsense. She is sure of that.

Part Two

Wilderness

Chapter 5

"Lady Ranger" at the Canyon

(Grand Canyon National Park)

bring back something from
the brink of nothing

—Chana Bloch

"Can you be here in a month?"

That question, uttered over the phone, was how I became a seasonal ranger at the South Rim of Grand Canyon National Park. After the earthquake, after my year of teaching ecology in the redwood forest, I drove the eight hundred miles into the wintry January desert to the Grand Canyon, my non-identifying information tucked away in my duffel bag, my stomach fluttering.

Unpacking warm clothes in my seasonal ranger housing—a trailer—I placed the pages in the back of a drawer in a dresser of hand-hewn pine that I was pretty sure was cast-off hotel furniture. I had still not discovered the reason for my aching joints and back pain, or, for that matter, anything more about my identity. For the moment, though, the pain had somewhat subsided, so I tried to ignore both the disease and the fact that I was adopted.

I brought Don with me. After a year of living and teaching together in the redwoods, we had decided to go afield on a different type of adventure and applied for ranger jobs. We moved into a shabby Park Service trailer known locally as The Dumpster because it was the same shape and dusty-green color as the waste disposal bins throughout Grand Canyon Village. Rumor had it that the trailer had originally been used as housing for the builders of Glen Canyon Dam in the mid-1950s, and it had been inadvertently submerged in floodwaters several times. It was now 1991, and The Dumpster was showing its age. But it had a strong furnace and double bed. And Don was there.

My job as a seasonal ranger was to stand behind the visitor center's front desk and answer tourists' questions. Some examples: "What are the road conditions from here to Alabama?" and "Where is the elevator to the bottom of the canyon?" and "Why are all the hotels full?" My favorite was "Is this the place where they have the presidents' faces carved into the cliffs?"

As park employees, we were obligated to be polite, no matter what a visitor said, but I found it difficult to keep a straight face when people asked such things. "You're a little south of Mount Rushmore," I said.

It was also my job to lead hikes along the canyon's rim and give talks about cultural and geological history, which I learned as fast as I could, poring over books about Ancestral Puebloans and geologic epochs in the Park Service's library and chatting up other rangers, trying to absorb their knowledge.

For the first time in my life, I was living very far away from my parents. I had always lived within a few hours' drive of my hometown in northern California, but now I lived almost a thousand miles away, and although I was trying to feel independent and adult, I got a twinge in my chest when I thought about how far removed I was from the people who knew me and loved me best. Worse yet, my parents had recently decided to split up. And my brothers were both away at school. It felt like our family was dissolving. Without my parents or brothers nearby, I began to feel like I had no family at all. The isolation of living on the snow-covered rim of the Grand Canyon in the dead of winter triggered something in me—I wanted to uncover things long concealed.

———————

When I was at work, Don, who didn't have a job yet, made a daily practice of hiking off-trail below the rim, collecting items that had blown or fallen off the lip of the canyon: shredded straw hats, vintage soda bottles, broken trail signs, animal bones. He displayed these ersatz treasures on our kitchen table like clues to a mystery we were trying to solve: What year was this soda bottle made? From whose head had this hat blown off? A ring-tailed cat's jawbone kept me company every day as I ate my Cheerios before hiking to the visitor center to field tourists' questions.

———————

Much like all that flotsam on our table, Don and I flung ourselves into the canyon's depths every weekend to explore it together on foot.

In January and February, we strapped claw-like crampons to the insteps of our boots for the first frozen thousand-foot descent from the rim.

In March, when it was forty degrees up top, we retreated into the canyon to camp at the river, where it was a comfortable seventy.

In May, we left our backpacking stove at home, thinking the weather would be hot enough to cook our freeze-dried beans without a flame. (It wasn't. We choked down blobs of watery, uncooked freeze-dried beans.)

For day hikes, we often found a way to descend on one trail, traverse a plateau halfway down the canyon, and meet up with another trail to hike back to the rim, tracing "U" shapes throughout the canyon.

Following these smaller canyons off the main channel, I began to learn the various personalities of each. The Tanner Trail followed a cleft full of huge limestone boulders that required hopping from one to the next; the New Hance Trail had narrow shale ledges near its top that forced us to face into the cliff, standing on tiptoes and shuffling sideways to descend to the purple-and-ochre-striped sandstone boulders at the bottom; the Hermit Trail's canyon felt boxed in and claustrophobic, but it had fossils embedded in the trailside sandstone that kept me company when I hiked alone; the bedrock of the South Bass Trail proffered secret potholes that we drank from when our water bottles ran dry.

On each hike, I searched for remnants of the Grand Canyon's cultural prehistory: ruins, granaries, rock art, potsherds. As I learned the trails, their geography told me their stories. And all that strenuous walking made my aching joints calm down for a while.

I had always been good at finding little treasures. When I was about ten, my family visited Yosemite National Park for the first time, camping in the valley with my aunt, uncle, and cousins. I had a crush on my handsome uncle, Bernie.

One afternoon, as everyone lounged on the pebbled banks of the Merced River with Yosemite's striated granite domes soaring above us, Bernie started to skip stones across the water. I appointed myself his personal rock-finding assistant, wanting his approval as a good helper and a good rock-skipper. We scoured the shoreline looking for skipping rocks.

"Here's the kind we need," he said, showing me a perfectly flat stone. "They have to be heavy enough to throw with a good spin, but not so heavy that they'll sink when they brush the creek's surface."

I nodded, my attention rapt. He flicked the stone he'd shown me—it slid perfectly across the river.

Soon I became an expert skipping-stone locator, amassing a pile of skip-worthy rocks faster than Bernie could throw them. Then, focusing intently, I tried skipping them, awkwardly attempting the wrist-flick he'd shown me.

He walked over to me and repositioned my arm. "You've got to really whip it over the water," he said, guiding my arm through the motion. My rock sailed and skipped a couple of times before sinking.

"Yes!" He squeezed my shoulder and smiled at me.

I smiled back at him, then grabbed a nice shiny stone for him to skip. As I offered it, I saw the rock had a peculiar shape and scrutinized it more closely. It was a chiseled piece of obsidian—volcanic glass, black and semi-translucent, the size of my thumbnail. The edges, once knapped to the keenness of my Swiss Army knife's blade, were now thick and dull. I ran my thumb around the edges, mapping its surfaces, and looked up at Bernie.

"It's an arrowhead," I whispered.

"You sure?"

I could hear the disbelief in his voice.

But I knew it was. This was a bona fide treasure, made and used by actual Native Americans. No one I knew had ever found an arrowhead, and even better, I now possessed one and my little brothers didn't.

I placed the arrowhead in his hand, saying, "See? It really is." Bouncing from foot to foot, I yelled, "Mom! Dad! Come see what I found!"

As my parents ambled over, my little brothers racing past them to get to me first, Bernie said, "You're right. It *is* an arrowhead." He set it back in my hand and ruffled my mop of hair affectionately. "You're good at finding things."

I beamed at him, rubbing the dulled edges of the small projectile point between my thumb and forefinger again and again, reveling in the texture of its cool, glassy surface.

In the Grand Canyon, hiking each trail offered new insights into its geological history, and I gradually began to understand that together, the many canyons formed one impossibly large entity, one large world itself; the process of exploring trails and artifacts became like seeking a family.

Descending and re-ascending thousands of vertical feet on those daylong or weeklong journeys was physically challenging work. I felt stripped to my most bare and vulnerable self as I hiked them, although the hiking itself required a certain toughness that I wore like a coat.

My joint pain hadn't disappeared, but it had remitted enough that I could usually ignore it. And it seemed to respond well to hiking. Trekking in the Grand Canyon gave me a light, hopeful feeling. I named it "That Expansive Canyon Feeling."

Washing dishes after dinner one night in our tiny trailer kitchen that had mystery chunks stuck to its walls from its many previous occupants' cooking endeavors, Don and I discussed our future together, once I finished my seasonal contract with the Park Service.

"I got my results from the GRE Biology Test today," Don said toweling off a saucepan. He had taken the exam just before we moved to the Grand Canyon.

I looked up from the sink full of soapy water and dirty dishes and asked him how he'd done.

He grinned. "I did really well. I think I'm all set to go to grad school."

"I'm so proud of you! Tonight, we'll celebrate!" I said, flinging my wet hands around his neck and hugging him.

"I'll apply to NAU," he said, putting his long arms around my waist and slow-dancing me around the cramped perimeter of the kitchen's linoleum floor. Northern Arizona University was only seventy miles away in Flagstaff. "I'm not sure what kind of biology I want to study. Maybe ants. Or birds—maybe I'll study the ravens in the Grand Canyon. I'll go to campus soon to talk with a few professors."

"Sounds good," I said, wondering how I would fit into his plans, feeling like the linoleum floor was slipping out from beneath me.

"Want to live with me in Flagstaff?" he asked, smiling and tickling my ribs. I batted his hands away.

"Yes," I said. "Maybe. What would I do there?" I knew Flagstaff a bit, having done most of my grocery shopping there while working at the canyon.

I had been thinking I might try to get a job as a backcountry ranger at the bottom of the Grand Canyon. I didn't like working at the visitor center: the lines of people waiting to ask their questions had gotten longer as summer approached. And I was sick of wearing a Smokey-the-Bear hat and clip-on necktie to work every day. They made me feel cartoonish, like the ranger in Yogi Bear shows I had watched as a kid. In fact, just the day before, a woman with a Texas drawl had spied me stationed on the rim in my uniform as I answered questions during the "Ask a Ranger!" program.

"Oh, lo-ok!" she exclaimed. "A la-dy ra-nger!" She ran up to me, pulled the wide-brimmed Stetson off my head, and jammed it down on her puffy blond coiffure. She yelled to her husband, "Ho-ney, take a pic-ture!" I felt my face get hot.

The man raised his camera, and the woman put her arm around me and mugged for the photo, still wearing my hat. I stood woodenly, feeling even more like a cartoon character than usual.

"I didn't know they had la-dy ra-ngers!" she said after he snapped the picture. "Do they al-low that here?"

With measured speech, I said, "Can I have my hat back, please?" and put out my hand to receive it. In my ranger training, I learned that as a federal employee, a representative of the US government, an ambassador of the Grand Canyon, I had to remain polite. But I could barely keep from lashing out. Her actions were rude and sexist, and they made me wonder what I was doing there. I was also angry because in the same way that she thought "lady rangers" weren't "allowed," I felt I wasn't allowed to know my own origins. How could I take myself seriously if I didn't really know who I was?

After a beat, the woman handed me my hat, and I pulled it on. "Yes, they do allow women to be rangers here," I said in a clipped tone. "They do in every park. Enjoy your visit." I forced a smile and walked down the trail to the visitor center, where I was due in a half hour to stand at the desk and answer more questions.

Could I work as a backcountry ranger and see Don every two weeks on my days off? I had also toyed with the idea of getting a job at Walnut Canyon, a small national monument just outside Flagstaff that drew fewer visitors.

Or maybe I could just get a job at the little vegetarian café near the NAU campus that served a noodle salad I loved. Maybe I could wear flowy skirts and let my hair grow long and be a groovy Flagstaff girl. I didn't know who I wanted to be. Part of me wanted to just tag along with Don, to let him make all the decisions. But another part of me knew that following Don's dream wouldn't make me happy. I needed a dream of my own.

Despite that, I said, "How about I get a job at Morning Glory Café?

That way I could find out what's in their delicious Thai salad."

"I could see you working there," Don said as he stacked dishes in a cabinet.

The wind whistled outside, shaking the trailer a little.

I tried to picture myself behind the counter at the café, away from the canyon, far from my parents, with Don, who would probably work in some biology lab twelve hours a day.

———————

I lay awake in bed that night, thinking about the kind of plans I wanted to make for myself. I wanted to search for my birth parents. Perhaps, I thought, it would be similar to a series of canyon hikes, a search that would loop closer and closer to the truth about my origins until I found what I was looking for. I desperately wanted to feel I could trust Don and make this move with him, but I sensed a lack of investment from him. He had his own plans, and I was ancillary to them.

———————

The next morning, after Don had left for his new job as a busboy at El Tovar, a fancy hotel and restaurant on the rim, I sat eating breakfast, my usual bowl of cereal settled alongside the ring-tailed cat's mandible. I grabbed the phone book and opened it to the Yellow Pages. Flipping through the A's, I found it. Adoption. There was an ad for ALMA, the Adoptees' Liberty Movement Association, offering free support for people touched by adoption interested in searching for biological family members. I stared at the entry as I nervously crunched on my Cheerios. Who would answer if I dialed that number?

Heart pounding, I called, and a woman answered. "Hello, this is ALMA," she said in a scratchy smoker's voice. "Lorraine speaking." She didn't sound like she was answering the phone for an official organization—she sounded like she was just someone sitting in her house smoking cigarettes.

"I'm an adoptee interested in searching for my birth mother," I said. Outside the trailer window, two ravens swooped between the pinyon trees.

"Do you have your non-identifying information?" she asked.

"Yes," I said, surprised. I had never heard anyone but the social worker from the adoption agency use that term before. Perhaps it would help me find my origins after all.

"Can you read it to me?" asked Lorraine, hoarsely.

"Hold on just a minute." I ran to my bedroom to retrieve the pages from my dresser and returned to the phone. As I read them to her, I could hear her pen shuffling across paper, taking notes.

"No last name, huh?" she said.

"No . . ."

"Well, that makes it tough, but here's what you can try for starters. It sounds like your birth mother's a hundred percent Norwegian, so your maternal grandfather probably belonged to the Sons of Norway Association." She paused and coughed. Her gravelly voice gave me unexpected comfort. "You can call the Sons of Norway clubs up in northern Colorado. Tell them you're planning a family reunion, but you've lost track of some of the people in your family. Say you're looking for a Norwegian family who lived up there in the 1960s."

Lorraine cleared her throat. I heard the scraping sound of a butane lighter igniting, then Lorraine's deep inhalation. I waited. She exhaled.

"Who are the Sons of Norway?" I asked, stalling so I could absorb what she was saying. I took notes as fast as I could.

"It's a club for men of Norwegian ancestry," she said. "Chances are, your family still lives up there."

I continued scribbling notes, excited and scared—this sounded like work I didn't have the guts to do.

"You should mention that you aren't sure what their last name is, but give them the approximate ages of your birth mother and her parents, and some of the details you just read me. Tell them you know the dad belonged to the Sons of Norway back then for sure, and maybe ask them to send you some photos or lists of names of their membership. That'll give you a lead on some possible last names."

"Okay," I said, struggling to write everything she said. Her plan sounded sneaky. I was not very good at lying, and cold-calling elderly Norwegian men in Colorado was not the kind of thing I was used to doing. "Thanks, Lorraine; I'll give it a try."

I must've sounded as tentative as I felt, because she said, "Call me back if that doesn't work. We can take another approach if we need to."

"Like what?" I asked, slipping the pages of non-identifying information back into the protective plastic sleeves I kept them in.

"Well, you could petition the court and tell them you're having heart trouble or something, and you need them to release your sealed information so that you can find out about your medical history. You could say you're worried you might have a life-threatening genetic disease."

"I do have an undiagnosed medical problem," I said, rubbing my lower back, where the pain had recently returned.

"Then maybe you want to try that route first."

"How?" I asked, feeling even more uncomfortable than when I was imagining lying to Norwegian old-timers. I wondered if I could I really go up against the court.

"You'd need to contact the Colorado State Juvenile Court and ask to petition for your sealed records."

"I can do that," I said, relaxing a little. Pursuing a legal route sounded much less scary. I wanted to find my birth family, yes, but I was too shy to actually go driving around trying to find them and talk to them. I wanted to find out who they were, but I didn't exactly want to be the one to find them. I wanted to feel safe.

"Give it a try, but keep in mind that Colorado's laws are very strict. They don't like to open adoption records, and they rarely do it at the adopted person's request."

I thanked Lorraine again and said good-bye. Again, I looked out the trailer's window. The ravens were gone now, and it was snowing hard. At least it was my day off, so I didn't have to trudge through the snow to the visitor center and answer questions. Today someone would definitely ask "Why is it snowing in the desert?"

I wondered if it would be helpful to get my adoptive parents to ask the adoption agency and the Colorado Juvenile Court for information on my behalf. Would they have more clout than I would? But I had not yet told my parents I wanted to search. I was afraid it would hurt them.

I wondered if they would understand my need to know. I wondered, given that they had recently decided to split up, if this news would make things worse in our already suffering family.

———————

I arranged a conference call with my parents a week later, telling them that I had something important I wanted to discuss with both of them at the same time. I wanted to draw them to me. I was so far away.

When all three of us were on the phone, I drew in a breath and held it. Silence. It was snowing again, a swirly, spring snow. I watched its movement through The Dumpster's window, still holding my breath.

"What is it, honey?" my mother asked.

"I want to find my birth parents," I said quickly, grabbing a lock of hair and twirling it around my finger like I had when I was a little girl. "Is that okay with you?"

"Well . . . sure," said my father, speaking slowly as if to be very careful of what he said.

My heart pounded—I didn't want him to think I didn't love him.

"Of course it's okay," my mother replied. Relief flooded my body. "I can check your baby book for the notes I took when the adoption agency called to tell us they had a baby for us, but I don't think we have much information. I was so excited that we finally got to have you that I didn't pay much attention to what they said about your background. I just remember writing down what kind of formula we were supposed to buy."

I wondered what the social workers had told her that, in her excitement, she hadn't written down. Could it have been a clue I needed that was now lost forever? I was happy that my parents seemed to understand my need to search but frustrated that they hadn't known, way back then, that the information the agency gave them might be important one day.

"Hey, kiddo, you'll always be our little girl," my father said, trying to lighten the mood. I imagined him sitting in the study of the little bungalow he'd moved into.

"Thanks, Dad," I said, distracted, mind racing. I tried again. "Do you remember anything about what they might have said about my birth parents?" My hand was poised above the notebook in which I had begun keeping search information, waiting to hear something that might help me. I stared at my thumb, wishing I still sucked it.

"I think they said your birth mother wanted to be a schoolteacher," said my mother.

"Yes, and I remember something about you being of French ancestry," my dad said. I knew this was incorrect—my non-identifying information said that my birth father was of Swiss heritage—that was probably what my father was misremembering.

I began to understand that mining my parents' memories for a particular day more than two decades in the past was going to be mostly fruitless, so I asked them about the court approach. They agreed to write a letter in support of my petition and to the adoption agency stating that they supported my search. We said good-bye, and I hung up the phone, stunned that I had actually told them I wanted to search and had asked them for help. They seemed not to be threatened by my interest in finding my biological parents, and I was grateful for that. But I wondered if they were hiding their true feelings for my benefit.

One thing was clear: they were not going to hold my hand while I searched. That was not how they parented. And I hadn't been able to ask the question I most wanted to ask: "Will you help me?"

For as long as I could remember, they had let my brothers and me do most things for ourselves. Sometimes I had liked that parenting philosophy because they had given me a lot of freedom and as a result, I had become quite independent at a young age. But other times the independence they granted me backfired, and I felt afraid, unsupported.

When I was nine years old, my friend Robin came over to my house one day, and we took off on an adventure by ourselves as we often did. We hiked along the creek a few blocks from my house to my favorite sycamore tree whose trunk jutted out over a riffle in an L-shape, like a person sitting cross-legged. Privately, I called it the Love Tree, imagining that, one day, I would sit in its lap with a boyfriend, our legs dangling into the creek ambling below as we held hands and smooched.

I didn't tell Robin any of that for fear of being teased. We hiked along a dusty path down to the Love Tree carrying empty Folgers coffee cans, trying not to cut our fingers on their sharp edges.

In the creek, we hunted water skeeters and scooped them into the cans. I loved to watch how their long slender legs made dimples in the water's surface without breaking its tension, a magic trick to bend water. We captured insects for what seemed like hours, wading in the creek below the dusty trail, engulfed in our world as captors of small creatures.

A young man came splashing down the creek wearing a brown T-shirt with silk-screened images of Charlie Chaplin and long pants. We noticed his black socks with prickly, walnut-sized cockleburs stuck all over them. He looked funny, walking in socks down the creek—we always wore sneakers or went barefoot. But socks? Robin and I stopped hunting long enough to catch each other's eye and giggle a little.

"Hello, girls," the man said, approaching us. He was skinny and pale.

"Hi," we said, unnerved as he intruded on our wildlife hunt. I averted my eyes and skimmed the water's surface with my cupped hands, catching more of the skeeters, and moving downstream a little to get away from him.

"Stay and talk to me, girls," he said.

Robin and I glanced at each other furtively. She looked as scared as I felt. "We were just getting ready to leave," she said.

"Stay and talk to me, girls," he repeated.

I picked up my coffee can and stood up, glancing over at him, preparing to walk away. He held a yellow pocket knife, sharp blade unfurled and glittering in the dappled sunlight beneath the trees. Terrified, I looked back over at Robin. She stared at the knife, transfixed.

"Sit down for a while and talk to me," the man said. "I'm in school to be a psychologist, and I'm supposed to talk to kids as part of my training." He remained in the middle of the creek.

We nodded and slowly sat down in the slurry of wet sand and pebbles on the shore. I settled my coffee can alongside my hip. Looking over at Robin, I noticed that her face was ashen. How would we get ourselves out of this situation?

"So, what would you like to talk about?" he asked, as if *we* had invited *him* to chat.

After a good bit of silence, I said, "I don't know." I didn't meet his gaze but looked at the knife, then down by my hand at a fist-sized river rock. I pried the rock from the wet sand and peered beneath it. A tiny dead fish floated in a puddle underneath. I crushed it, squishing its guts out and mashing it with the rock. The rock uttered soft thuds.

"Should we talk about sex?" he asked.

I felt my face go red, and my stomach turn. I dropped the rock and gathered my knees close to my chest with my arms.

Robin and I both looked down at the smashed fish. Its intestines curled out from its belly, floating in the puddle.

I didn't want to talk about sex. And I did want to. Every fourth-grade kid kind of wants to talk about sex, but not with a grownup. Especially not with a grownup holding a knife.

I shrugged.

At that moment, my friends, Rain, Mary, and Buzzy rode by on their banana-seat bikes, beach towels slung around their necks, zooming toward the nearby public swimming pool.

I yelled and waved at them, "Hi, guys!" I hoped they'd stop and rescue us from the guy with the knife. The guy who wanted to talk about sex with a couple of nine-year-old girls. "How's it going?" I yelled, giving them a pleading look with my back to the scary man, trying to send them a message with ESP: *Please stop! Help us! We're in trouble!* I waved hard.

I glanced at the man and noticed he'd hidden his knife behind his back.

My friends did not stop. They zipped away, yelling hellos to us. They obviously had not received my ESP message.

Robin and I were stuck. The man pulled his knife out and began cleaning his fingernails with it. We sat back down. I resumed smashing the dead fish with the rock, avoiding eye contact with the scary man.

"So, you begin by fondling each other's private parts," he said.

Oh, God, I thought, *he's really going to tell us all about it.* Why did he want to talk about sex? What would he do next? How were we going to get out of this? I turned my head to look over at Robin, desperate to make an escape plan with her, when I saw something moving on the trail. It was another man: tall, stocky and sunburned, smoking a cigarette, walking quickly and looking around.

It was Karl, Robin's dad, and he looked angry. He often looked that way, which usually made me scared of him, but at that moment I was overjoyed to see him.

I dropped the fish-smashing rock loudly into a puddle. Robin's dad heard it plop. He looked down and saw us by the creek.

"What the hell are you girls doing down there?" He growled. "It's late! I was supposed to pick you up a half-hour ago, and I've been looking everywhere for you!"

I peeked over at our stocking-clad captor, who had judiciously pocketed his knife. He was scrawny, and Karl looked imposing, standing on the trail. He was not a man to be messed with.

"Let's go, girls!" he called. "Hurry it up already!"

Without a word to the knife guy, Robin and I grabbed our cans of skeeters and scrambled up the stony embankment.

Robin called up as we climbed. "Sorry! We lost track of time!"

When we reached Karl, I turned to look at the creek. The man with the knife was gone. My heart pounded. I was still scared, but now I was angry too.

Karl looked like he was about to cuss us out. He took a deep drag on his cigarette. His face was red and sweaty. When he exhaled, smoke enshrouded his head.

"That guy pulled a knife on us!" Robin said, gesturing to where the strange man no longer stood.

Karl regarded us for a beat and, seeming to ignore her accusation, said, "Come on. Let's go."

We followed him, trying to keep up with his brisk clip along the trail. I wondered why he didn't believe us, but I didn't dare talk back to him.

Ten minutes later, we arrived at my driveway. Karl told Robin to get in the car and lock the doors, and he told me to tell my parents what had happened. He then jogged back in the direction we had just come from.

He had believed us, after all, and it looked like he was going to find the guy and deliver some vigilante justice.

I walked into my house and told my parents, who hugged me and said we needed to go immediately to the police station to file a report.

On the way out the door, I saw Karl returning from his manhunt.

"I couldn't find the guy anywhere," Karl told my parents as he opened the driver's door of his muscle car. He was panting. I gave a small wave to Robin, who was still inside the car. Karl started the engine and roared off down our street.

Relieved that my parents were taking the situation seriously but rattled from the experience, I felt guilty, as if my ambivalence about listening to the scary man had somehow prompted him to talk to us about sex. I hadn't said, "No, don't talk to us about sex!" I felt complicit and dirty.

Did I explain any of this to my parents or the police? No. I didn't even mention that he had started to tell us about "fondling each other's private parts," a phrase I had never heard before, and I have never since forgotten. Instead, I sat in a scratchy upholstered police station chair thinking about the opaque eyes of the dead fish I had ground to a pulp at the creek.

When we returned home, I emptied the cans of muddy water and skeeters into the gutter in front of my house and watched the helpless insects float through the sewer grate. And in the bathtub that night, I scrubbed slimy creek mud from my shins, fish guts from my hands, sand from my hair. Finally, I reclined in the slightly murky water and sucked my thumb for comfort, trying to reconnect to the universe.

My parents had trusted me when I told them what had happened, but they hadn't been there to help me when I needed them. It was ironic that Robin's dad had been there, as he was usually absent when I visited her house. But that day, he had saved us from who knows what.

To my knowledge, my parents had never read any of the research about the psyches of adopted children or adult adoptees. Like most people involved with closed adoptions in the 1960s, they were ignorant about the psychological trauma babies experience when separated from their mothers, how those babies may grow into children who feel that they don't belong, that they have been abandoned, that there is something intrinsically wrong with them.

Back on the South Rim of the Grand Canyon, snow swirled outside my Dumpstery little trailer. I grabbed my backpack and my instep crampons, and I headed to the rim to descend through snow into the springtime that lay hidden in the warm depths of the canyon. Somewhere down there, claret cup cacti bloomed blood red, and I, the Lady Ranger, was going to find them.

Chapter 6

Ruins and Ladders

(Navajo National Monument)

Love is a word another kind of open—

—Audre Lorde

After I told my parents I wanted to search, we sent letters to the adoption agency and the Colorado Juvenile Court, asking for information about my birth parents. We emphasized the importance of learning my medical history because of the as-yet unidentified chronic illness I suffered from. In return, we each received a letter from the juvenile court:

```
All adoption records are closed upon finaliza-
tion. A court order demonstrating 'good cause'
is required to release information. The infor-
mation in adoption and relinquishment matters
in Colorado is confidential and the court is very
strict in this regard. Having a good cause hear-
ing in no way guarantees that any information
will be released to you.
```

A door had slammed in my face. I was furious. How could the State of Colorado have more rights than I did to information about my birth, my family? It didn't seem right, but I didn't know what to do about it.

Before I completed my contract as a seasonal ranger at the Grand Canyon, my mom flew out to visit me. I wanted my parents to visit me together, as they had always done, but now they were divorced and that wasn't going to happen anymore. I was reluctant to face facts.

During my mom's visit, I wanted to take her on an overnight hike to the Keet Seel ruins in Navajo National Monument. These ancient dwellings lie at the end of an eight-mile hike through undeveloped land, and I had obtained a special permit months in advance to camp there and visit the ruins.

The day before we were supposed to hit the trail, my mom and I checked into a roadside motel during a thunderstorm in a tiny town on the Navajo reservation. We dashed into the motel's office through a heavy downpour and rented the last room available, a non-smoking room.

When we got to our room, I unfolded the topographic map of our route to the ruins on the floral-patterned bedspread. She pulled up a chair next to me, turning on the nightstand lamp as she sat.

I traced my finger along the dotted line marking the trail. "We'll start on this plateau at 7,300 feet and descend into the canyon. There'll be switchbacks for the thousand-foot drop. Then we'll hike through this creek bed for about six miles." I pointed to the braided blue line marking the meandering stream. "We'll end up over here." I showed her lines indicating a side canyon that housed the ruins and the small backcountry campground where we could pitch our tent.

After studying the map a moment, my mom stood and pulled back the motel drapes and peered out the window at torrents of rain. She lit a cigarette.

I was annoyed but not surprised that she had decided to smoke in the non-smoking motel room.

"I'm flattered that you think I'm strong enough to do that hike," she said, tapping ash into a glass on the nightstand. "But it sounds too hard for me. Plus, if it's going to keep raining like this, I don't want to spend the night camping in the wet and cold."

I had hiked with my mother before, even took her backpacking once. We hadn't hiked far, and I carried most of the weight to help ensure that she would enjoy the experience and want to go again.

I really wanted to see the Keet Seel ruins, and I really wanted her to see them, so I had convinced myself that she would be able to do it. I didn't want to go alone. I wasn't prepared for that. I had asked Don to join us on our road trip, but he declined and instead made plans to climb a sandstone spire near Monument Valley while I was away.

"Are you sure?" I asked. "I think you can do it. I could carry most of the stuff." I added, even though I could easily imagine an unpleasant scene on the trail: her becoming angry with me for pushing her beyond her limits.

"Let's see if there's some other way for me to get there," she said, blowing smoke and tapping ash into the glass again. I wrinkled my nose.

I picked up the telephone to call the backcountry office at the park, cancel one of my hiking permits, and ask how we could get my mother to the ruins. The ranger I spoke with said there was an equestrian outfitter who led trips. So my mother reserved a spot with a tour on horseback to visit the ruins for the day. That meant I would hike alone and camp for the night by myself. I had backpacked a lot, but always with Don. I was going to have to go without him this time.

I missed him, but ever since he had started talking about graduate school, cracks had begun to form in our relationship. My doubts about his commitment to me had made me distance myself from him emotionally.

Recently, on a climbing day, I stood in the red dirt at the rim of a small canyon near Flagstaff, watching him rig an anchor around a humongous ponderosa pine. He deftly tied into the rope, and off he went, backing his way below the canyon rim, feet against the pocked basalt. He sailed down the rest of the way, like a flying squirrel flitting from treetop to forest floor. Seconds later he stood at the bottom of the canyon and unclipped from the rope. "I'm off rappel! Your turn!" he yelled up to me.

I stood on the rim in the morning's slight breeze. The seed heads of dried grasses rattled a little, echoing the sound of the wind. I fastened all the buckles on my harness and threaded the rope through my belay device, clipping it into the harness. Don and I were the only people there, and up top I felt very alone. I had rappelled a hundred times before, but I never liked it. I didn't trust equipment, even though I knew Don backed up his anchors and backed them up again. To lean back into airy space at the top of a crag always felt unnatural to me, like agreeing to fall off the edge of this world that I so desperately wanted connection to.

I held the rope taut beside my hip, ready to feed it out as I backed down the cliff, feet against the dark stone. I leaned back, but I was paralyzed with fear; I couldn't release my grip on the rope and my heart pounded.

"What's up? Aren't you clipped in?" Don called.

I paused, biting my lip and trying to figure out what was happening, why I was having an existential crisis at that moment—or was it a panic attack? Or both? I tried to lean back again, but again something stopped me.

"I can't do it." My voice echoed along the basalt corridor.

"Is something wrong with the anchor?" Don asked, a little exasperated.

I shook my head although I knew he couldn't see me from below the lip of the canyon. I was trying to shake something out of it—my fear or the idea of rappelling, I didn't know which. "No, the anchor's okay," I said. My weight was still heavy against the back of my harness, hand still cinching the rope. I wasn't quite standing, not quite hanging. Limbo.

"Well, what? Let's climb before it starts getting hot," he yelled. I could hear the impatience in his voice.

I lurched forward, up to the ponderosa anchor, catching my weight on my feet instead of against the rope. "I can't do it," I yelled down to him.

"What's the matter?" he hollered, sounding annoyed.

I worried a section of the rope between my fingers, its black fibers woven with neon pink and green strands. It was kind of furry—Don called it "Count Fuzzula" for its wooly appearance. It wasn't exactly frayed, but I wondered how safe the rope really was. Don had a strange sensibility of what was safe and what was not—sometimes he seemed overly concerned with it, other times rather reckless.

"I just can't rappel. I don't want to." I was tired of scaring the shit out of

myself rappelling and climbing, especially with him: he was so much better at it than me that his expectations of my performance were impossible.
He always pushed me too hard, convincing me to rock hop down steep
gullies, climb overly difficult pitches, and hike across snowfields without
ice axes when we really should have had them. I always ended up cracking
my knees against granite, slipping off climbs, sliding down ice fields, and
ending up bloodied and scabbed, sobbing and cursing him. I had just now
realized I wasn't willing to do it anymore just to spend time with him.

"Why didn't you tell me you didn't want to rappel before we drove all
the way out here and set up?" he yelled, his anger echoing in the bottom
of the canyon.

"I didn't know this was going to happen!" I stepped away from the
rim and unclipped the rope from my harness, relieved that I wasn't going
to rappel or climb but anxious about what would happen next with Don.
He loved nothing in the world more than climbing, and I was standing
between him and the object of his desire. At the time, I didn't understand
I'd had a panic attack, and I certainly didn't have the words to explain.

"Toss me one end of the rope. I'll need you to belay me from up there
while I climb," he said in the dispassionate monotone he used when he
was angry.

I lowered him one end of Count Fuzzula, threaded the other end
back through my belay device, and clipped the rope into my harness
again. "You're on belay!" I yelled. I could hear him scraping the pebbles
off the bottom of his climbing shoes, preparing to set his toes into the
cliff's tidy dihedrals.

"Climbing," he called. Still monotone.

My stomach ached. We had driven all the way out there, and I was
refusing to climb.

"Climb away," I said. "I can belay you from up here as many times
as you want." I couldn't see him. "Today doesn't have to be a washout." I
called.

He didn't respond.

In a few minutes, his shaggy head appeared, and soon he stood on the
rim, unclipping from the rope. "Off belay," he said automatically, looking
down at his harness as he unbuckled and stepped out of it.

"You're off," I said, repeating the rock-climbing protocol. "Why are you taking off your harness?" I asked. "You can still climb—I'll belay."

"Let's go," he said. "This isn't worth it." He collected the rope and started coiling it.

"I'm really sorry," I said.

Don finished coiling the rope and slid it into its nylon bag. Without a word, he untied and removed his climbing shoes, dropped them into his pack, and reached for his sneakers. Anger, maybe even disgust, radiated from him like heat from a sunbaked stone. Beyond what I'd already said, I couldn't explain what had happened to me. All I knew was I couldn't make myself rappel, didn't want to climb with him anymore. In the silence, I felt something slip away.

I loved him. Needed him. Most of my wilderness identity had been developed with, and perhaps because of, him.

Yet I couldn't inhabit that persona all the time; she wasn't everything I was. There was also the person I had grown up as: oldest child, good girl, straight-A student. And there was the identity I hadn't found yet: one that Lorraine from ALMA was trying to help me locate, one whose absence terrified me and kept me up at night wondering if I could possibly become anyone if I never knew my origins. Or what would happen if I did.

We finished packing and drove home through tall ponderosas. I apologized a few more times, said I was just having an off-day, that I didn't feel well. He grudgingly forgave me, and we stopped on the outskirts of Flagstaff for a belated breakfast of scrambled eggs slathered with New Mexico green chile. But a shift had occurred. I doubted I would ever rappel into a canyon again just so I could climb back up it, and I knew I had to continue paying attention to the yearning I felt to pursue the leads Lorraine had given me. I also knew I would have to do that without Don.

———

But on the road trip with my mom, I missed Don. I missed the closeness with him, I missed his expertise in the wilderness, his sense of wonder at the natural world, his willingness to try anything.

———

When my mom dropped me off at the trailhead, I hugged her good-bye and hoisted my big green backpack onto my shoulders. She drove off to find the stables where a horse waited to carry her. As I hiked down from the mesa, I noticed a vertical pattern of handholds and footholds running up the steep sandstone of the trailside cliff. It was a ladder of sorts. I couldn't see where it led. I wondered about it as I hurried on, eager to get to the ruins.

When I reached the canyon bottom, I trudged along, crossing and recrossing a stream. My mom's equestrian group caught up with me after an hour or two, and we leapfrogged back and forth for miles.

One woman on horseback was writing a travel guide to the southwest. When she took a picture of me mucking through the stream wearing my big pack, I imagined my likeness published in a travel guide. I hoped to look brave and strong in it as I hiked in solitude among the sandstone spires. I tried to inhabit that image of myself.

Mostly, though, I was lonely, even among the formations that rose from the bedrock in anthropomorphic shapes. I named them to keep my mind busy: Corn Mother, Three Muses, One Woman Standing. The names echoed my footsteps as I plodded along.

In the early afternoon, I watched my mom's brown-and-white spotted horse trotting ahead of me and thought about how my family was changing. At Christmas, just before I had begun working as a ranger at the Grand Canyon, my youngest brother had opened a gift, an indoor weather station, and I made a joke about it.

"Is that for when you need to know the weather inside your house?"

"You're such a brat!" My mom said, frowning—I had insulted her gift.

Again, trying to be funny, I said, "*You* raised me."

"I guess I wasn't the right woman for the job." Her eyes welled.

Breathless, I tried to think of a witty response to her barb to diffuse things, but I couldn't. It hurt too much.

"Why do you have to be so tough about everything?" she asked.

My toughness was a shell protecting my insides, which were fragile as newly formed skin beneath a scab. How could she not know that? And what incentive did I have to let down my guard when I knew it would be met with her anger when I was trying to make a joke? Did she not know her comment would fuel my feelings of displacement?

Long before that Christmas I had told her, "I feel like I wasn't wanted, Mom."

"But you *were* wanted—you were so very much wanted by us." She didn't understand that I felt abandoned, given away, expressly *not* wanted.

On the trail, a small herd of cattle stood in front of me, tails twitching. At first I wasn't alarmed, but then I saw a bull standing still, nostrils flared and sharp horns pointed toward me.

How did I appear to him? Tall, green, and scary wearing my big pack, I hoped. But I feared I looked like a small, foolish woman, worth chasing and goring. I bent laboriously under my pack's weight and picked up a rock, held it tightly as I walked in a wide arc around the bull. He let me pass. But I gripped that stone for the rest of my hike.

A few hours later, I arrived at the trail's end. The ranger's hut, a hexagonal, juniper log building made to look like a traditional Navajo hogan, hunkered in the shade of nearby cliffs.

I saw my mom's group finishing their tour of the ruins. They walked toward a picnic table below the cliff, and I, tired, sweaty, and fixated on the cheese and crackers waiting somewhere in my pack, joined them to eat.

"I'm so glad we found a way for me to get here," my mom said when I caught up with her. "It's amazing in there." She smiled, gesturing behind her toward an alcove in which many ancient sandstone buildings were visible. "So many rooms and artifacts! I saw a thousand-year-old corn cob next to a grinding stone!"

"I'm glad you liked it, Mom," I said. "I can't wait to go in there. I wish we could have gone together." I wanted to share the experience with her, to be together when we encountered the relics, the empty wind blowing through the crumbling buildings.

After lunch, she gave me a hug and left on horseback with her group. "See you tomorrow at noon," she called, riding off down the wash.

That was the plan we had made. And now I had ahead of me almost twenty-four hours of being alone. I sat at the picnic table trying to decide what to do first, pitch my tent or visit the ruins, when two tired hikers shambled up to the picnic table and dropped their packs heavily on its bench.

I looked up to say hello and was surprised to see people I knew— Stew and Charlotte. He was a well-loved ranger at Grand Canyon, famous for his evening programs at the South Rim in which he did a slapstick routine, making a great show of impersonating Grand Canyon pack mules and the tourists who rode them to the bottom of the canyon. Stew's wife Charlotte, fit, forty-something, was a historical archaeologist at the Canyon.

"Fancy meeting you two here," I said, smiling at them from my seat on the bench.

"Andrea!" Stew said. "What a surprise!" His long, craggy face cracked into a toothy smile.

At that moment, a guy about my age wearing a park service ball cap strolled up and introduced himself. "Hi, folks. I'm Mike, the ranger here. I can take you up to the ruins in a few minutes, if you'd like."

Stew introduced himself and said, "That'd be great. Would you mind if we ate some lunch first?"

"No problem," Mike said.

"Please, join us," said Charlotte. Mike sat down at the picnic table with us, and Stew and Charlotte pulled out some sandwiches. I opened my water bottle.

"All three of us work at Grand Canyon," Stew said, gesturing around the table. "One of our friends in Archaeology told me to ask you about some nearby ruins—not far beyond Keet Seel, I think she said."

Mike said he knew of them and offered to take us there first thing in the morning since we were fellow park service employees. I was happy to be included, and I wondered what we'd find.

Mike took us on a tour of Keet Seel, the largest cliff dwelling in Arizona, a huge settlement with kivas, or circular ceremonial chambers; many sandstone buildings with wooden ladders leading from one level to another; and thousands of objects from daily life seven hundred years ago in the desert southwest: pottery, corncobs, grinding rocks, and stone scrapers. Although it had been abandoned for centuries, the village looked as if the population had departed just days before.

———————

I didn't know what move I would make next in my quest to find my birth parents. Petitioning the adoption agency and Colorado's Juvenile Court for information hadn't worked, so I would have to take a different, probably sneakier, approach. I liked the idea of hiring a private investigator, but I didn't have the money for it.

Wandering around ruins like Keet Seel made me begin thinking I could search on my own, as Lorraine from ALMA had suggested.

After touring the ruins, I hiked to the campsite and set up my blue backpacking tent and shared a dinner of spaghetti and ginger candy dessert with Stew and Charlotte. I noticed the same cattle that had startled me while I hiked were now grazing throughout the camping area. I hoped that they were afraid of tents, or at the very least, that they would avoid stepping on mine while I was in it.

As the evening wore on, it became clearer to me that I didn't like doing backpack trips alone. For one thing, there were too many decisions to make on my own: where to pitch the tent, how much to worry about being trampled by cattle, how high to hang my food from hungry rodents; the list went on. Stew and Charlotte were camped a good bit away, out of earshot, which made me feel even more alone.

In my little tent that night, missing Don, I distracted myself from my preoccupation with the cattle by envisioning the footholds and handholds I'd seen chopped into the gritty Kayenta sandstone during my descent into the canyon that day. Known throughout the desert southwest as Moqui steps, they are prehistoric pathways, climbing routes carved by the Ancient Puebloans. I knew it was important to leave any archaeological artifact alone so that it might be preserved and appreciated by future generations. But were the steps artifacts? All I knew was that they called to me. I desperately wanted to put my hands and my feet into their small recesses to see how they fit, to find out where those hanging cliff trails would take me.

On my travels, I always wanted to venture a little further than I knew I should, to see what might be there. Those handholds spoke to that urge. I fell asleep listening to cattle hooves thudding around my tent, chopping their own footholds in the desert sand.

I awoke in the morning unharmed.

I had told my mother I'd hike out first thing so I could meet her by noon on top of the mesa, but I wanted to see the secret ruin with Stew and Charlotte. I knew my mom would worry if I didn't make it by noon. But I couldn't convince myself to skip the opportunity to see something that most people didn't get to see, especially since I had hiked so far with my heavy pack. So I decided to go with the group to see the turkey ruins, as they were known, then hike out of the canyon as fast as I could.

After breakfast, Mike led us up an arroyo to a place where pictographs of large birds were painted with brown and white pigment on the canyon walls. He pointed to a row of sticks aligned vertically near the cave's wall. "The Ancestral Puebloans kept turkeys for eggs and meat, and the archaeologists think this was where the birds were caged."

Stew, Charlotte, and I wandered around the small ruin quietly, looking at pictographs and remnants of turkey fences. I was lost in thought about what it might have been like to live there tending turkeys.

Mike cleared his throat and said, "There's a skull—a human skull—sticking out of an arroyo down canyon from here."

I looked up at him, body frozen in place. Charlotte and Stew had also stopped in their tracks and were staring at Mike.

"What?" Stew said.

"I'm not sure what to do about it. If I tell the Park Service, they'll probably launch an archaeological trip to catalog it and stabilize it—or unearth it," Mike said.

"Yes, that's probably what would happen," Stew said, leaning on his hiking pole. He had worked for the Park Service for a long time and was well acquainted with its bureaucracies.

"The thing is," Mike said, taking off his olive drab ball cap and wiping his sweaty head, "I don't want the skull to be disturbed."

"I agree," said Charlotte. She was sitting in the shade, her back against a boulder, a wide-brimmed hat obscuring her face.

"I don't know," said Stew, shifting his weight to his other hiking pole. "All kinds of things might happen to it if it's left alone."

"Can we see it?" I asked. I could barely contain my excitement, but I tried to act casual, as if I saw skulls on all my hikes. I had never seen a human skull outside of a museum before, a skull in its sort-of-native habitat.

"Yes, it's just down that wash a piece," said Mike, pointing to a dry streambed left of the turkey cage.

We walked about a half-mile down the pebbled arroyo, and Mike stopped and pointed up the embankment to an unmistakable white orb buried about five feet below the scant desert topsoil. It was obvious that the skull would soon become completely exposed and roll to the bottom of the arroyo, where it would be washed away with the next storm or crushed by the hooves of a cow looking to graze. I wondered about the rest of the skeleton lying behind the skull and pictured it, too, eroding out bone by bone. Who was this lost person? Ancestral Puebloan? Navajo? Cowboy? Cowgirl? Hiker? I presumed the skull was very old, but I had no evidence of that. It was buried in a floodplain. Perhaps it had been dislodged from its original resting place only a few years before, then buried by a flash flood's silt and sand like just another stone in the riverbed.

I'd seen my share of backcountry oddities, but the skull got to me in a new way. It was lost, possibly disembodied. It had to belong somewhere, to some family.

Like Mike and Charlotte, I wanted that skull to rest where it lay. It seemed right to let it fall to the creek bed and move along as the forces of gravity and erosion took it.

Similarly, I wanted to preserve the integrity of the ancient toe-and-handhold ladders, but I yearned to fit my hands and feet into them, to use them as they had been intended. Because what is a foothold if it's not used? Where does a route lead if no one hikes it?

Also, of course, I wanted to locate the bones, and the flesh, of *my* ancestors; I wanted to follow a path that would lead me to the place where they lived, as if they had just stepped out one day to get the newspaper and had never come back, where the idea of me had been abandoned. I wanted to fill those holds with my feet, trace them with my shoes, have someone else's to fill.

———————

Eventually we left the skull, and our little party split up. My three companions loped off to explore even more ruins, and I jogged back to camp to shoulder my pack and hustle out of the canyon to meet my mom. I was eager to tell her about my bonus adventure, and a little nervous that she'd be angry for making her wait in the desert worrying about my safety.

After miles of walking through the stream's quicksand, I arrived at the base of the final ascent. The Moqui steps stared at me, leading my gaze up. They took a more direct route than the trail, which was switchbacked for hikers and horses. I knew I shouldn't try the Moqui steps that day. The weight of my pack would throw me off balance. There was no one there to catch me if I fell.

Instead, I scuttled up the final grade as quickly as I could. When I finally topped out, sweaty and tired, heart racing from exertion, back aching from the weight of my pack, there was my mom, waiting for me, just as we had planned. I was about a half-hour late, but she was smiling as she stood on the windy mesa-top waving to me as I approached. Relief flooded my body when I saw her smile.

"Hi there, strong woman!" she called.

"Sorry I'm late!" I said, dropping my pack in the gravel as I reached her. I gave her a big sweaty hug. "You're never going to believe what I saw!"

"I'm sure you had quite an adventure," she said, chuckling. "You always do."

Perhaps she had expected my lateness. I wondered for the first time how she had kept from worrying all the times I told her I was going into the backcountry for a week, two weeks, a month, and that I would call her when I got back to civilization. Maybe she had worried, but she'd let me go anyway, without a fight. Or maybe she hadn't worried, perhaps only because she didn't know the potential dangers.

As we got in the car and drove back to the motel, I told her about the secret ruin and the skull and the handholds.

"I really wanted to climb the Moqui steps! It was hard not to do it."

"I can tell!" She replied. "Frankly, I'm surprised you *didn't* climb them. You're like the bear who went over the mountain to see what she could see."

The children's song ran through my head: "The bear went over the mountain to see what he could see." She was right. That was how I felt about all my backcountry trips, and also, of course, about finding my birth parents. I needed to know what was out there. Even if I found skeletons.

But then I remembered the last part of the song about the bear: "all that he could see was the other side of the mountain . . . that's all that he could see." Was all I would find "the other side"? Would that be enough?

I was compelled to ask her something I had been too scared to bring up when we talked on the phone about my search. It was as if it were a physical need, like inhaling after holding my breath for too long. "Is it okay with you that I want to search for my birth parents?" I looked down at my lap and picked at my cuticles.

Silence.

"Yes," she said, staring out over the steering wheel at the wide, thunderhead-filled sky. "It seems important to you, and I want you to be happy."

"I don't want you to feel threatened by my need to find them," I said. "You and Dad are my parents. You always will be."

"I'm glad you feel that way. That's how I feel too. Even though your dad and I have split up, we're still a family."

I wanted to believe her. But our family had changed. All five of us now lived in separate houses. My brothers and I were young adults. I wondered what family really meant. Especially now that I was searching for another family.

I thought about the skull and the Moqui steps. What did those artifacts mean to me as a hiker, a ranger, an observer? Was it my right to decide how they would or wouldn't be used, whether they would or wouldn't be handled? Did I have the right to disturb the past? If not, who did?

Chapter 7

Crumbling Steps

(Grand Canyon National Park and
Navajo National Monument)

Today to the end of the marvelous stair,
Where those glittering pinacles flash in the air!
Climbing, climbing, higher I go,
With the sky close above me, the earth far below.

—Amy Lowell

When I returned to the Grand Canyon after the trip with my mom, I signed up with the International Reunion Registry, the Adoptees in Search National Registry, and the Colorado Voluntary Adoption Registry, all organizations that help reunite long-separated family members seeking one another. I wrote to each registry, explaining where I was born and when, and I included the little bits I knew about my heritage—Norwegian ancestry, birth mother born in 1949, birth father in the irrigation supply business somewhere in Colorado. Once the people who worked at the registries received my letter, they would use a database to see if my information matched that of others who had registered.

Within a month, I received replies from all those registries—there were no matches. No one was looking for me.

When I got the news, Don was away again rock climbing, somewhere in Utah. In the twenty-four years since I had been surrendered for adoption, no one had made the effort to search for me. I felt like I might vomit. I wondered how it could be true that no one wanted to know who I was, if I was all right, happy, or, at the very least, alive?

When Don returned from his climbing trip, he was dirty, tired, and happy. And I was embroiled in my search. After receiving the bad news from the registries, I had called an independent adoption searcher in Colorado, who said, "If you don't have a name, I can't help you." Her comments exasperated me—she was supposed to be the search expert, not me.

"Why is this so hard?" I slumped on the couch in our trailer, ignoring that Don had only been home an hour or so.

He walked over and sat down next to me on The Dumpster's polyurethane couch.

"Maybe you just need to go up there—have a look around," he said, rubbing my back. He hadn't had a shower in days, and he smelled like fear-sweat from climbing, but I nestled into him anyway.

Putting my head on his shoulder, I let out a frustrated sigh. I stared down at his dusty black climbing pants. He wore them almost every day, whether he was climbing or not. He had patched the knees twice, using blue thread that stood out against the worn black fabric. I sighed again, tracing my finger along the river of blue thread, mapping it.

The next day I took Lorraine from ALMA's suggestion and looked up Norwegian surnames in Grand Canyon Village's tiny public library: Amundstatter, Brekstad, Christiansen, Dahl, Eriksen, Guttomrmsen, Henriksen, Isaksen, Johnnesdatter, there were many more. Which one was mine? How would I find out? I didn't know what to do with the names, so I wrote them down.

I wanted to go back out into the wilderness to take a break from figuring out how I might find my birth name. The skull in the arroyo and the Moqui Steps beckoned me back to Navajo National Monument. I told Don about Keet Seel and the skull, and he wanted to see them too, but we didn't have a permit. We hadn't yet visited Betatakin, a cliff dwelling two miles into another canyon in the park, so we decided to go.

The trip would kick off our last few weeks together before I flew to Alaska. I had decided to take a training course to become a wilderness guide, so that I'd have options for outdoor employment in the future. I would spend five weeks in the Alaskan backcountry on a guide training course, during which I would kayak, backpack, and traverse glaciers, all while learning how to lead groups on wilderness trips.

Upon arriving at Navajo National Monument, Don and I pitched our tent in the tiny primitive campground that Edward Abbey portrays in the scene in his eco-warrior novel, *The Monkey Wrench Gang*. His three main characters camp there while plotting and enacting an elaborate plan to blow up a nearby coal-conveying bridge in the name of environmental justice. Don was an Abbey devotee who had done some monkey-wrenching of his own before I met him, and when we were first dating, he read aloud to me the least offensive passages of Abbey's unapologetically sexist and racist books. I didn't love Abbey's tired tropes: the male gaze, the male desire to possess women, the male need to possess the wild. But I was secretly thrilled to camp at the place where reality and fiction intersected, where literature and landscape collided. *The Monkey Wrench Gang* was fiction, but I knew that Abbey and his friends had carried out acts of civil disobedience like those described in the book—pouring sand in gas tanks of giant earth movers, tearing surveyors' stakes from the soil, all in the name of preserving the wild.

I pictured Abbey himself camping right where we placed our sleeping bags and writing by moonlight while sitting at the very picnic table where we boiled our spaghetti noodles, where later, at dark midnight, I wrote in my journal the misgivings I harbored about my future. I wanted to be a wilderness guide and was going away to get trained, but after that, I didn't have any plans. I only had a vague notion of starting my own wilderness travel company for women. I wanted to provide a supportive way for women to enter that male-dominated landscape, not the way I'd learned with Don, scrapping my way up mountains and crags without knowing how to use my equipment, struggling to keep up because he was so much more experienced than I was that he didn't even know what I needed to be taught.

Beyond that, my idea of starting a company was inchoate. I knew nothing about running a business. I knew I wanted to work outside, but I wasn't sure my health condition would allow me to do the kinds of things I wanted to. I still didn't know exactly what was wrong with my body, and while I no longer needed the heavy-duty medication, I was often in pain; I woke up stiff and achy every morning, and my back hurt all the time. Would my body hold up to the rigor of the training and guiding I wanted to do?

And what about Don? I loved him, but I needed more partnership from him than I was getting. He had a plan for his life—grad school, fieldwork in biology—and he was happy to have me tag along, but I would just be a hanger-on. I wasn't sure I wanted that. I already felt so lost, I didn't want any more identity crises.

———————

Visitors are only permitted to see Betatakin on a guided tour with a ranger, so the next morning we took to the trail with a big group. The ranger knew Mike, the Keet Seel ranger. As we hiked down the steep trail in the morning shade, I mentioned I'd been down to the turkey cave ruins a few weeks earlier, had seen the skull in the arroyo.

"Mike told me about that." He flashed a smile. "I want to dig out that skull, stick a candle in it, and put it on my coffee table."

I'm sure my disgust showed on my face. I reconsidered my previous opinion about leaving the skull alone; maybe it would be better if the park archaeologists removed it rather than risking the possibility of it falling into the hands of someone like that guy.

I slowed my pace and waited for the ranger to trek ahead to answer questions for other hikers, who were pointing at a far-off alcove.

I pulled Don aside. "That guy is a jackass!" I said. "Let's get away from him."

Don smiled. I adored his crooked teeth, his always-scruffy beard. "Let's check out the ruins," he said.

A large, deep alcove sheltered the ancient village of Betatakin. Don and I hiked up to the alcove wall to a pictograph: a large white pigment circle enclosing an anthropomorphic form. Its hands gestured, trailing something: Light? Magic?

"Is it welcoming us or warning us away?" I asked Don.

He shifted his backpack's weight. "I don't know, but it's super cool," he said.

The candle-in-the-skull ranger walked up behind us as we inspected the big white pictograph. "That's the Hopi Fire Clan symbol," he said.

"What do you think it's doing with its hands?" I asked, pointing to the tracers around the figure's arms.

He lifted his Park Service cap by its brim, repositioned it. "I don't really know. But have you seen the pictographs of handprints and bighorn sheep over there by that crevice?" He pointed to a crack beyond the Fire Clan man's waving arms.

"Nice," Don said, nodding. We moved toward the handprints to escape the ranger.

We wandered among masonry rooms whose forms echoed the rectangular boulders around them. As always, I marveled to see the centuries-old wooden ladders and even a few ghostly-gray, completely intact pottery vessels.

Our hiking group began to head back up the trail away from the ruins, but Don and I hovered behind. He pointed up at the canyon wall. "Let's go climb some Moqui steps."

I didn't want to climb with him anymore, but I did wonder what it would be like to remove my shoes and grasp the first handhold on the rock face. I imagined taking my time to fit my fingers and toes into each little alcove, climbing the cliff's stone ladder, the pink sandstone grainy and warm beneath my skin. I pictured this place without rangers, without rules, with only the pleasure of moving up stone in search of something ineffable.

But I declined. Don frowned at my refusal to climb. More and more, I needed reassurance that Don was unable to give me. Probably no one could have provided me with the kind of affirmation I needed. I wanted him to say, "I will never leave you, I will always be with you, I will always love you," the kind of commitment that came into question right after I was born. I had learned by then, after being left behind by various boyfriends, that it was easier to do the leaving than to remain and risk being left. I wasn't sure what I would do about my relationship with Don, but I thought being in Alaska for a big chunk of the summer would help me figure it out.

I hadn't left my search behind. I had spoken again with Lorraine from ALMA. She told me I should try to talk to someone at my adoption agency, ask questions about my birth mother that would help me search: *What did she study in college? Was she from Colorado's eastern plains? What is the first initial of the name of the town they lived in? Is the town known for something?*

I couldn't imagine having that kind of conversation with a social worker. What if she denied me any information? What would I do then?

But Lorraine had given me a few ideas that I could imagine working on. "Find out if there are scholarships given by the Sons of Norway," she'd said. "Look for your birth father based on the fact that his father owned an irrigation supply company."

I thought about how I might do that.

"Find high school yearbooks with swim team pictures to find your birth mother," she continued. "You could also call the Denver Veterans of Foreign Wars to try to find your maternal grandfather and look up wedding announcements from September 1966 to see if you can find records of your birth father's marriage to the other girl."

It seemed like a goose chase to me—and overwhelming. I didn't know if I could do it or where to start. Like the Moqui Steps, I was unable to just grab a handhold of the search and start climbing. I was afraid of what I would find when I topped out.

Chapter 8

Double Vision

(Flagstaff, Arizona)

her fine blades making the air wince

—Adrienne Rich

We returned from our trip to Navajo National Monument to Don's new place in Flagstaff. He had paid the deposit for his first semester in grad school and rented a house near campus. During the countdown to my leaving for Alaska and the start of his classes, we squeezed in one more adventure together: a day hike up Humphreys Peak, Arizona's tallest mountain.

Although the route up Humphreys was steep and talussed, Don and I navigated it easily. We were both strong and accustomed to the rugged terrain of the high country. I looked like some mountain man's girlfriend, and sometimes, that's all I felt like, my blond ponytail braided against the wind, hair flying like dandelion fluff around my face, sunburned nose. It was easy to hide in Don's shadow, to let the world knock on his door first. Despite my tough exterior—over-muscled legs from hiking, callused hands from climbing and handling ropes—I was thin-skinned. My sense of self was tattered from the obstacles I'd faced trying to find my birth parents, and what little confidence I still had was shaken. Seeking people who perhaps didn't want to be found, and who apparently didn't want to find me, was something I could only do with peripheral vision—if I looked at it head on, I felt I would disappear.

At the summit, the view was clear: we could see a hundred miles south to the Verde Valley, where we had once slept out on a hillside, watching the mysterious ascent and descent of green-striped aurora borealis rays. I had never seen them before in my life, their electric curtain rising and lowering throughout the theater of night. Since seeing the Northern Lights from Arizona is very rare, I felt that something important was happening. I just didn't know what that something was.

Up top, standing in a snow patch, I gazed out at almost every place we'd hiked together in Arizona, except, of course, the inner gorge of the Grand Canyon, which is always hidden until you hike into the guts of it. That view was a timeline of our past year together.

Don extracted his camera from his pack and snapped our obligatory top-of-the-mountain-shot: camera held at arm's length to take a picture of our smiling faces, necks craned toward each other. (The word "selfie" hadn't been invented yet.) There were several other people on top of the mountain, each performing similar summit rituals with cameras, plus one man who seemed to be talking into a radio. I noticed him and wondered why a person would struggle all the way to this peak only to talk to someone far away. Such were the days before cell phones.

It was windy, so we donned the few extra articles of clothing we'd brought for the day, thermal shirts and rain shells, and hiked a half mile along the ridge to get a view into the old volcano's crater.

Standing on the rim and looking down into the snow and rock expanse, we saw a group of teenage guys tugging at something in the snow. Giant inner tubes lay like huge black donuts around them. "Looks like someone's hurt," I said. My heart beat quickly, and I made no move toward the figures in the snow.

I saw Don's body stiffen. We both watched in silence for a long moment. "We'd better go down there," he said, eyes still trained on the commotion below us.

"Yeah, we should," I said. But I didn't want to. I feared a gory scene I wouldn't know how to deal with.

Yet we both took off glissading down the slushy snow to the group of guys.

They were trying to drag a boy to dry ground. All appeared to be in their mid-to-late teens. And they all had crew cuts, which made them look military and tough. I took a step backward.

"You guys need some help?" Don asked.

The tallest of the bunch approached us, breathing heavily. "We're trying to get our buddy off the snow," he said in a southern accent as he jagged his thumb behind him toward the guy lying on the ground. The kid they were dragging had blue lips, and I saw blood curling through his sand-colored hair.

"We were up here sledding on those tubes, and Mark crashed into some rocks down there," the guy said, angling his head to indicate the wet black crags below them.

Don and I helped carry him to the shelter of a small rock outcrop, and the tall guy introduced himself as Bert.

Mark was conscious, but obviously in shock: his blue eyes looked dull and sleepy, his body lay limp. His jeans and sweatshirt were completely soaked from the snow. The crewcut guys swarmed around their buddy, drawling protectively, not doing much else.

I stood back watching, feeling small and mute, thinking maybe they could take care of him. I considered turning around and hoofing it back down the mountain. I had recently gotten certified as an Emergency Medical Technician, but I wasn't sure I was good enough at actually practicing it to take on such responsibility.

A small group of the crewcuts tightened their laces, preparing to run down the mountain to get help. Don and I poured most of the water from our bottles into theirs so they wouldn't get dehydrated as they descended. Moments later, they took off down the mountain.

As I stood with Don on the trail watching the injured kid's friends hustle off, a pair of middle-aged hikers strode up to us and asked what was going on. When we told them, one offered us a fist-sized nylon sack of emergency supplies: a shiny silver space blanket for instant warmth and a striking-flint for lighting fires. I mentally inventoried the contents of my own daypack: a rain jacket, some sunscreen, and, now, only half a quart of water. No food, no headlamp or flashlight, no first-aid kit. Not very smart for an Emergency Medical Technician. I was definitely not prepared.

Don interrupted my thoughts. "Andrea, *you're* the EMT here—*you've* got to take care of this."

I didn't want to. I was used to Don pushing me; he had done it often during our years together, many times compelling me beyond my physical limits. But this time I knew he was right. He looked at me expectantly, eyes bloodshot from the high-altitude sun and wind exposure, his curly, unwashed hair blowing against his head as if an aerial tide were coming in.

I turned to face the first task: to convince a dozen teenage boys to remove all of Mark's sopping wet clothing and begin warming him with their own bodies.

"Okay, you guys—" I stopped and cleared my throat so I could yell over the roar of the wind. "We're going to have to get all his clothes off and get him into dry things, so crowd around him to make a barrier from the wind, all right?" I pulled my jacket around me for courage as much as warmth.

Soon, Mark was stripped and in dry clothes. His friends huddled, rewarming him. I gave them the space blanket to hold in any heat they generated. Mark wasn't bleeding much, but when I touched his neck and spine, he winced in pain. I could see him trying not to cry out.

Inside my head, I chanted: *Head injury. Neck injury. Blue lips. Passive demeanor. We've got to get this guy out of here.*

The wind blasted us as the sun crept downward. The guys whispered to me, "Is he going to be alright?"

It was quickly getting dark and cold. I remembered the guy with the radio. Maybe he could help. I asked Don to look for him. He grabbed his jacket and jogged up the mountain.

I returned to the teenagers and pulled Bert aside to tell him what I'd sent Don to do. Then I checked Mark's breathing, pulse, and level of consciousness as I'd been taught in my EMT course: rapid respiration, thready pulse, somewhat listless. Meanwhile, I tried to figure out what I was going to do if Don came back with the radio man.

I thought asking for a rescue crew on foot was too risky: it was getting dark and cold, with all of us at nearly 13,000-feet elevation with almost no water and even less food. If we didn't get out of there fast, we were all going to become hypothermic. And I didn't know how extensive Mark's injuries were. He seemed relatively stable, but I didn't want to take any chances. I thought we needed to get him helicoptered out to safety.

Don and the man with the radio appeared, walking down the path toward us. I jogged over to meet them. The man already had the sheriff's office on the line. I had barely learned how to work a radio from when I was a ranger, even though I had carried one around on my belt during ranger hikes.

"There's been an accident on top of the mountain," I said. "A teenage boy—fourteen years old. Possible C-spine injury. He's bleeding from his head." My hands were cold. I wanted to shove them back in my armpits.

"I'll send up a rescue crew on foot," a dispatcher said through static. "They should be there in three or four hours."

I held my breath for a few seconds. "I think we need an air evacuation."

"Really?"

"Yes. I don't think he can wait much longer."

"Okay, I'll call for a helicopter. Stand by for further information, Humphreys." That was me—Humphreys.

I thanked him, wondered if I was doing the right thing and what the consequences would be if I wasn't. I stood on the ridge fifty feet above the crewcuts huddling around Mark and watched them all for a moment. They looked like a tiny swarm, a blurry bee's nest. My stomach hurt, I could feel my pulse thumping rhythmically in my temples, I was scared and thirsty. The evening was getting colder and windier.

The dispatcher's voice returned. He needed to know exactly where we were on the mountain, how hard the wind was blowing, and from what direction. I gave the best answers I could, again worried about what would happen if I were wrong.

Then a medic came on the radio. I could hear rotor wash in the background.

I told him Mark's condition in my best Emergency Medical Technician's voice, "Pulse one-twenty, respiration fifteen. Sledding accident: Head injury. Possible spine injury. Patient is semi-alert and oriented. Pupils are equal and reactive to light. Slight cyanosis around mouth. Spine painful to touch. Bleeding from head. Treating for shock and trying to keep him immobile. Over," I said, trying not to forget what I'd learned in my EMT class.

"I don't know who you are, Humphreys," he said, "but you're doing a great job."

I smiled a little, somewhat relieved. Maybe it was the right thing to call in a helicopter.

The pilot came on and confirmed our location and wind direction. "Hang a pair of rain pants or a rain jacket from a bush to give us a wind indicator," he said. "Pack everything into your backpacks and weigh them down with rocks. Tell everyone to lie flat on their bellies when we approach and cover their eyes from the dust. No one can be standing—there can't be anything that might fly up into the props."

We did the best we could, battening down everything except for someone's red rain pants, which became a windsock. Then we all lay prone on the dirt and waited for something to happen.

Soon we heard the aircraft whumping its way toward us, and it landed exactly where they told me they would. I looked up, squinting against the heavy wind from the rotor blades.

A man in a jumpsuit appeared in the doorway of the helicopter and beckoned to me. I ran toward him through the incredible noise. He brought out a gurney, and we belted Mark into it, carried him to the helicopter, and secured him inside. The blades continued to whirl loudly as we worked, eclipsing almost all other sound. The medic yelled thanks. Five minutes after it had landed, the helicopter lifted off again and disappeared into the encroaching dusk.

We all stood for a moment, stunned. I had assumed Don and I would ride in the helicopter too. With hardly a word to each other we all headed down the mountain. The crewcuts barreled straight downhill, cutting switchbacks to get to the hospital quickly.

Don and I didn't have headlamps, so we took the trail to be surer of our footing in the darkness. I trotted wordlessly, listening to my breath's percussion. Soon I watched boulders and aspen trees duplicate every time my feet hit ground. We had been at high elevation all day. I had been worrying and problem solving, trying to be brave and smart. Now, descending more than three thousand feet as fast as I could, my body began to fail.

When we reached Don's car, I had double vision. I hunched over and vomited. Back at his house, my head hurt so badly that I couldn't drink or eat anything, so I lay in the dark with a wet towel over my eyes, replaying in my mind all that had happened on the mountain, wondering what was happening to me.

I had become another victim of the accident, the primary thing I had been taught not to do in my basic first-aid class. I felt stupid and scared. How long would the effects of dehydration and altitude sickness last? Would I be able to go on my Alaska trip? Would Don take care of me? I knew he would make sure I was all right, but I also knew he would not take care of me in the way I deeply longed for. I tried to picture the Northern Lights, but I couldn't conjure up anything but darkness. Instead I had the same feeling of distraught resolve as when I decided not to rappel off the canyon edge. I wished Don could cure my lack of confidence, heal my feelings of inadequacy, erase my old fears and scars. But I was beginning to understand that only I could do those things for myself. I needed to take responsibility for my own life, my own decisions.

I awoke the next morning feeling hungover—headachy and brain-addled, but with normal vision. I turned my head to stretch my sore neck and saw Don sleeping beside me. Reassured by his presence, I pictured how the crewcut guys had banded together the day before like a colony of bees. They seemed to belong deeply to one another in a way that I craved. I slipped my arm around Don's warm shoulder and fell back asleep.

Later, I drove to the hospital in Flagstaff to see Mark. He told me he had three broken ribs. The big gash on his head had needed a bunch of stitches but he would be released from the hospital the next day.

I left the hospital feeling a little better—perhaps because seeing Mark confirmed the rescue had been a success. But where was my colony of deep belonging? The thought of leaving for Alaska was almost as painful as last night's headache. Don and I had been together in so many challenging situations, I sometimes felt like an appendage of his. Now we would have no contact for five weeks. I would have to cleave myself from him. I had told him that after the expedition, I would move in with him in Flagstaff, but I sensed I needed my own plan, something besides waitressing at a groovy café and being his girlfriend.

———————

Back when Don and I had watched the Northern Lights in the Verde Valley, I thought they might be a sign that we were meant to be together, that magic happened when we were a couple. But now I thought the important thing about the Northern Lights was that they were telling me to stake a claim on my own life. To knock on my own damned door. That important thing was about stepping out into the world, not staying behind.

I had bought a one-way ticket to Alaska.

Chapter 9

White Courtesy Telephone

(Talkeetna, Alaska to Cassiar, British Columbia)

press back that area in the west where no one lived,
the place only your mind explores.

—William Stafford

Summer waned, the fireweed gone to seed a sign of impending autumn. My wilderness guide training course was over, and my friend Marci and I went to a bluegrass festival near Denali National Park in the little town of Talkeetna. Soon she'd return to her job as a naturalist on an Alaskan cruise ship, and I would need to figure out a way home.

The festival turned out to be more of a biker convention than a down-home music gathering, so Marci and I kept to ourselves, away from the mostly male festival goers. On the final evening, we sat away from the stage under some trees and I pulled a cook pot out of my pack and began mixing dry tabouli and water. Out of the corner of my eye, I saw a tall, beefy guy with long blond hair dancing bouncily in the crowd. I wondered what kind of biker worth his Harley would dance that way.

But he wasn't a biker, he was someone I knew from home: Brad, a fellow naturalist from my year teaching in the redwoods. And next to him was Chip, another naturalist friend. That kind of coincidence happened to me all the time. I ran into people I knew in remote places so much that I had begun to expect it.

"Brad! Chip!" I had to yell to catch their attention over the sounds of ferocious bluegrass fiddling mixed with death metal guitar riffs.

Brad stopped dancing and looked around, trying to figure out who was calling him. He saw me and called Chip. They squeezed through the crowd, and we all hugged.

"What are you doing here?" Brad said. The two of them looked like big blond bears.

I introduced them to Marci, and we all walked down to the riverbank so we could hear each other.

"We've been in Seward gutting fish on the slime line at a cannery all summer. Heading home in a few days," said Brad. "Gonna drive the Cassiar Highway."

"You're not taking the Alcan?" I asked. I had heard that the Cassiar was rugged and narrow, unpaved in some places. The Alaska-Canadian was a safer route but longer by many miles.

"Yeah, it's shorter," Brad said, "and there are fewer cars on it. Plus, I'm gonna drop Chip off at his folks' place in Washington on the way back to the redwoods."

"Do you have room in your car for me?" I asked. "I could help with the driving, and I've got lots of tabouli to share!" I held up my cookpot.

Brad looked at the pot and shrugged. "Sure, you can ride with us. We're leaving at the end of the festival. You can drive a stick, right?"

I could.

It was a plan. It was time for me to go, and I was relieved to have a way back to the lower 48, although I didn't know what I'd do next. Don and I had broken up right before I left for Alaska, so I wasn't going back to Flagstaff.

I hugged Marci before she drove away from the festival to go back to work and packed my backpack to stuff into Brad's car. I waited for them at the festival entrance, and they drove up in a blue SUV with two mountain bikes strapped to the top of it. The car was packed with items from their three months of itinerant living. I was glad I only had a backpack to contribute. I hopped in and off we went, Brad taking the first driving shift.

We had driven a few hours southeast of Anchorage and were cruising along listening to a bluegrass mixtape of Brad's when I looked out the front windshield and saw a tractor-trailer coming toward us in our lane. I watched it, assuming it would shift back into the opposite lane as it saw us, but as it neared, it remained in front of us. Brad swerved off the highway and bumped along a ditch beside the road to avoid being hit.

He slowed the car to a halt. "What the fuck was that?" He was breathing hard, and so were Chip and I. We were all shaken, and I realized I should gird myself for this road trip.

Later, we stopped at one of the few roadside gas stations along the Cassiar Highway to stretch our legs and switch drivers. It was my first turn at the wheel, but before taking it, I mixed up another batch of tabouli in my cook pot. The tabouli needed a half hour to set, so I wedged the pot between my backpack and a box of cassettes in the backseat near Chip so he could reach it if he wanted some. I refilled my water bottle at the gas station spigot and took the driver's seat, settling my bottle next to me.

The Cassiar Highway is a wilderness experience in itself, remote and wooded. Brad, who sat up front next to me, grabbed the box of cassettes and inserted Bob Marley's *Greatest Hits* as Sitka spruce trees, willows, and fireweed whipped by us outside. Ahead on the left was a dark lake whose waters lapped at the edge of the highway. I shifted into fifth gear, dislodging my water bottle from the console between the seats, and it rolled onto the floor near my feet. I reached down to pick it up.

When I looked back at the road a moment later, the SUV was veering slightly to the right, heading off the road. Remembering Brad's difficulty handling the car when he'd had to drive off the highway to avoid the tractor-trailer, I quickly pulled the car to the left to get it back on the road. But I pulled too hard, and now we were heading straight for the lake at fifty miles an hour. Alarmed, I pulled the wheel back to the right, hard, trying to get us back into our lane.

The car rolled, then rolled again.

Backpacks, boots, camp stoves, and a guitar flew everywhere: in front of my face, out the windows, into my lap. The shoulder belt strained hard against my left collarbone as my side of the car hit the road, and I felt searing pain as we skidded on the road on my shoulder. Gravel scraped the car, metal bent and popped. We all yelled obscenities. Especially me.

The SUV came to a stop, its tires spinning innocently. Bob Marley crooned.

"Fuck!" Brad yelled. "What the fuck?" He was suspended by his seat-belt above me. I looked up at him, dazed. Bob Marley kept singing.

"Are you okay?" I said.

"Yeah, I think so." Then we both looked at the backseat. There was a jumble of duffel bags, backpacks, Birkenstock sandals, and books, with little white and green flecks of tabouli covering it all. We couldn't see Chip.

"Chip!" I yelled.

Brad yelled for him too. There was no response. Starting below my rib cage, a prickly sensation spread through my body. Had I just killed Chip?

I yelled his name again. Still no response. "We need to get out of the car and dig him out!" I said.

Brad was still suspended above me. "Chip!" he yelled, his eyes fixed on the pile of junk in the backseat. "Talk to me, man!" He unbuckled himself and climbed out the smashed passenger window above him. I unbuckled myself too and tried to climb out, as if from an underground cavern, but was stopped by a crunching feeling of my left collarbone grinding against itself. I knew it was broken. I reached up with my good arm, and Brad grabbed it and pulled me out of the car. My vision went yellow with pain.

Bob Marley was singing about jammin'.

"Chip!" Brad yelled. We stared at the tabouli-covered mess in the backseat, listening for a response from Chip.

A groan emerged. I was relieved that I hadn't killed him but still terrified that he was paralyzed or something. Brad and I rushed over to the car to dig Chip out. The tires spun. Bob Marley kept singing.

"Can you turn that off?" Brad yelled, reaching into a smashed-out window and trying to move aside some of the things that were piled on Chip. He threw a cooler, a twelve pack of beer, a duffel bag, and a tent out onto the pebbled road. My left arm was useless now, but I reached into the front of the car with my right and turned off Bob.

The forest was silent for a moment, then I heard the crunching of gravel under car tires. A car pulled up behind us, and I hurried over to it as Brad continued unearthing Chip.

"We need an ambulance! Call 9-1-1," I said to the driver. He nodded and turned his car around to head back toward the gas station we'd come from.

I returned to the smashed SUV. Brad had extracted Chip, and they were sitting on the side of the road.

"My back," Chip moaned. He winced and slowly lowered himself to a supine position. My heart sank again. Something was very wrong.

I teared up. "I'm so sorry, you guys."

"Don't worry about it right now," said Brad. "We need to get Chip some help."

"I sent the guy in that car to call an ambulance," I said. "I think we need to treat Chip for shock. Can you get him a sleeping bag to keep him warm?" I saw Brad look at my left shoulder. It was shiny with blood, and bits of gravel were embedded in it from where we skidded along the road. "I can't really carry anything. I think I broke my collarbone."

"Broken? Shit. I'll get you a sleeping bag too," said Brad.

We waited in the almost-spent fireweed alongside the road, Brad and I talking softly to a woozy and grimacing Chip, trying to distract him from his pain. After about an hour, an ambulance arrived, and its volunteer crew of one—a tall skinny guy—emerged and loaded the three of us into it. He drove us to the nearest hospital, which was in the tiny asbestos mining town of Cassiar, British Columbia.

After X-rays, Chip and I were admitted to the hospital and given its two patient rooms. Brad, who had emerged unscathed from the crash, was allowed to occupy the maternity room since it was empty anyway. All told, we filled the hospital.

My X-rays indicated that I had indeed broken my left clavicle. Chip's ailments, however, were harder to diagnose. His X-rays revealed no broken bones, yet he was in excruciating pain, and big bruises had formed on his lower back. The doctor determined he had injured tendons and ligaments, and that he would recover. It was just a question of how long it would take and what kind of treatment he would need.

I retreated to my hospital room and sobbed, knowing I was responsible for injuring Chip and destroying Brad's car plus the mountain bikes on top of it and the various items that flew into the lake when we rolled. And I was responsible for stranding us in a remote area of northern British Columbia. I cried with relief that I had not killed anyone.

I must have been making quite a bit of noise because the nurse came in and asked me if I was in pain. "No," I said, "I'm just . . ."

"I understand, dear," she replied. "It's a lot to deal with. Hold on a second, I've got something for you." She slipped out of the room and returned a moment later carrying the clothing I had been wearing when we crashed. They had hastily cut off my orange tank top and sports bra in order to X-ray my collarbone, and this nurse had sewn them back together.

"Here you go, I thought you might want these back."

"Thank you," I said, and began to cry again. I could not bear her kindness, nor that of the staff who had allowed Brad to stay in the hospital for free, nor of the strangers on the highway who had loaded our things from the SUV's wreckage into their own cars and delivered them to the hospital. I also cried about how awful I felt amid all that kindness.

She put her hand on my unbroken right shoulder. "Why don't you go visit your friends? You'll feel better."

She helped me out of bed and walked me to Chip's room. I wiped my face and put on a fake smile before knocking.

"Come in," Brad said. He sat in a chair near Chip, who was propped up in bed with several pillows.

"Hey, I've got something for you," said Chip, chuckling, then wincing in pain.

I couldn't imagine what he might have, since all our belongings were smashed, sunk in the lake, or sitting in the corner of my hospital room. Before I could ask him, he threw a handful of something at me, which skittered across my face and neck like grains of sand.

"It's tabouli," Chip said. "I've been finding it all over myself."

We both laughed, but gingerly because of our injuries.

"How are we going to get home from here when they discharge you guys from the hospital?" Brad asked.

I had been wondering the same thing. The car was totaled, it was being towed to some junk heap, and I had paid the hospital my last hard-earned four hundred dollars in cash for my stay there. "Let me call my parents," I said.

――――――――

The only phone was in the hallway. I dialed and listened as it rang. My mom picked up. "Mom, it's me, "I said. "I'm in Canada and I've been in a car accident. I'm okay, but I have a broken collarbone."

My mom inhaled sharply.

"I'm glad you're okay," she said. I could tell she was trying hard to hold herself together. "What happened?"

"It was my fault. I was reaching for my water bottle, and we went off the road. It was terrible!" My voice shook. I tried not to cry, wanting to show her that she didn't need to worry about me. But I continued, "The car rolled, Mom! It was so scary!" I started to cry. I needed her. I hadn't been able to talk to Brad and Chip about the crash. I felt too terribly guilty. There was no way I was going to ask them to comfort me.

"Oh, Pumpkin," she said. I heard my dad get on the other extension—he always went to her house for dinner on Sundays.

"Hi, Dad," I said and sniffled into the phone for a few moments, unable to speak. I pulled myself together and asked, "Can you guys help us get home?"

"Of course," he said. "Where are you?"

I felt tremendous relief to have someone else taking over after the events of the crash. Fatigue swept over me. I was exhausted from being on the run from my own feelings all summer long.

――――――――

Chip's mom was a travel agent, so my parents called her, and they figured out how to fly the three of us out of Canada. But the nearest airport was in

Whitehorse, several hours' drive away, and there was no public transport that would take us there, nor was there a rental car agency or even a taxi service. I figured we would have to hitchhike.

———————

Later that afternoon, as I rested on a chair in Chip's room, the nurse who had sewn my clothes back together walked in to take Chip's vitals. "Is there a gas station or something around here where we might find someone going toward Whitehorse?" I asked.

She looked up at me, her dark eyes shining. She had an angular face and black hair, but there was a softness to her. "I'll drive you to Whitehorse when my shift is over."

"Oh, no, that's not what I meant," I said.

"I would want someone to do it for my kids if they were stranded in the States," she said and smiled, patting my back a little. I looked at Chip, stunned. We, the walking wounded, would not have to hitchhike hundreds of miles.

She left the room, her uniform's skirt swishing gently.

"Thank you!" I called.

———————

That afternoon, after she finished her twelve-hour shift at the hospital, she loaded us and the gear salvaged from the crash into her car and drove us the five hours to Whitehorse.

Halfway through the journey, she stopped at a gas station to fuel up. We tried to slip twenty-dollar bills into her hand to at least pay for gasoline.

"I won't accept your money," she said, waving the cash away.

We thanked her repeatedly.

Hours later, when we arrived at the airport, she helped unload our luggage from the trunk of her car outside the terminal. "You be safe now," she said, smiling, and gave us each a hug. Then she drove away.

———————

The three of us boarded a plane to Vancouver, where Chip's parents were waiting to pick up Chip and Brad and drive them home to Bellingham,

Washington. I had to take another plane to get to California. It was almost midnight when we arrived in Vancouver, and my next flight was scheduled to leave at six the next morning. I said good-bye to Brad and Chip, apologizing over and over as they hugged me carefully, avoiding my broken left side. I watched them walk to the curb to meet Chip's parents.

My left arm hung in a sling, my shoulder bare and flecked with road rash and scabs. Bruises and more scabs punctuated my forehead and cheeks where the car's shattered windshield had sprayed me with glass. I steeled myself to endure the next six hours, waiting in the airport. As I walked toward the international terminal, a woman and her young daughter hurried past me in the opposite direction.

The little girl pointed at me and said, "What's wrong with her, Mommy?"

I tried to smile at her.

"Shhh," the mother whispered to her daughter, "It's not nice to stare at people who look like that!" She took the girl by the hand and steered a wide berth around me as if I were toxic.

I walked on. An announcement came over the loudspeakers. "Andrea Ross, please go to a white courtesy telephone for an important message."

Puzzled and a little apprehensive about what the message might be, I found one of the white phones, picked it up, and identified myself.

"Your transport to the hotel is waiting for you at the curb," someone said.

"I don't have a hotel reservation."

"I have a message here that says your family has arranged for you to stay in a hotel until your next flight, and you are to meet a van outside that will take you there."

I hung up the phone, bewildered, and hurried out to the curb, where a driver stood in front of a hotel van holding a placard with my name inked on it.

He drove me to a hotel, one of the nicest I'd ever stayed in, and helped me up to my room. "I'll be back in four hours to take you back to the airport, Miss," he said, and left me alone in the spotless room.

I barely held myself together until he left, carefully lowered myself onto the bed, and cried again.

After breaking up with Don, I had arrived in Alaska, numb and raw. I learned to lead people through tundra and forest, across bodies of water, over glaciers and up mountains. One night, as I lay alone on a pebble beach in Kachemak Bay gazing at the sky from my sleeping bag, I felt a familiar sense of oneness with all those stars. It happened every time I slept outside. I telescoped between feeling minute and alone and feeling utterly connected to all of it. Spending four hours in that clean, quiet hotel room was another kind of comfort, one provided with love from my parents.

Chapter 10

Dancing in Quicksand

(Montezuma, New Mexico
and Grand Canyon National Park)

And I asked myself about the present: how wide it was,
how deep it was, how much was mine to keep.

—Kurt Vonnegut

After Alaska, I got a job in northern New Mexico as a wilderness guide. The small international school that hired me was nestled at the base of the Sangre de Cristo Mountains, overlooking the Great Plains. My students were smart, ambitious eighteen- and nineteen-year-olds from all over the world, and since the school was located in a wild, remote area, it had a focus on wilderness as well as academics. My job was to guide them on wilderness trips and teach wilderness search-and-rescue methods.

During our long trudges up mountains, across snowfields, and into canyons, I listened to my students discuss their plans and dreams. They wanted to teach each other about their respective cultures, to solve global political problems and public health issues, and to effect change as policymakers, health practitioners, professors, United Nations envoys. I was in awe of their purposefulness and focus at such a young age.

One night, we were camped on the South Rim of the Grand Canyon. My boss Kenneth, the head wilderness instructor, called us together for a final talk before we departed on our routes early the next morning. We bunched up, sitting on the crunchy pine needles and dried grasses of northern Arizona's autumn as the sky grew dark. Kenneth lit a camp lantern whose blaze glared off his round eyeglasses.

He and I had very different views about wilderness trips. He subscribed to a military model: always be on guard, see wilderness as your adversary. I saw wilderness travel as an opportunity to understand the natural world, to find commonality, not difference.

"You've all worked hard to earn a spot on this trip," he said.

At the beginning of the school year, Kenneth had insisted that everyone who wanted to go on the Grand Canyon trip run three miles with him three times a week at six in the morning for the month before the trip. The students had hated getting up so early to go running, but they did it because they wanted to go on this once-in-a-lifetime trip, and I did it because I wanted to keep my job.

"You only have to get up at the crack of dawn one more time for this trip," Kenneth said.

A collective groan rose from the students.

"You've proved you're strong and tenacious." Kenneth grinned toothily, looking like a sea monster. He ignored the groans. "But the canyon is a dangerous place. There are many hazards out there."

I looked toward the canyon reflexively but saw nothing more than tree shadows cast by Kenneth's lantern. An evening breeze brought the dry smell of pine. I glanced around. Some students looked alarmed, others' eyes had glazed over with boredom. A few shifted in their spots on the cooling earth, as if their legs had gone numb from sitting.

"Everyone must stick together on the trail." Kenneth licked his lips and smiled his monster-tooth smile again. "The canyon is big and more powerful than you. You need to fear it."

I couldn't sit silently while Kenneth disparaged the place I had felt was a home, a touchstone, a refuge ever since I lived there as a ranger. "Can I add something?" I said. I worried Kenneth would deem my comments disrespectful, but I couldn't stop myself. "What Kenneth's saying is true." Now the night air grew cold, and I shoved my hands between my knees for warmth. "We need to be careful while we're hiking and make good decisions with our free time while we're in the canyon because we don't want anyone to get hurt. The canyon may seem scary, but it's also the most comforting place I've ever been. I used to live here, and every time I've hiked into it, I've felt enclosed in welcoming arms."

A few students nodded.

"Thanks," Kenneth said, his voice a bit strained. "I think it's time for everyone to get some sleep." He licked his lips again. I was beginning to understand it was a nervous tic.

I approached Kenneth after everyone had shuffled off to their tents. "I hope I didn't overstep." It was getting even colder. I shoved my hands into my armpits.

"It's all right," he said, "I just worry about their safety—they're kids, you know."

I agreed, but I was troubled that he would send them into my beloved canyon with hearts full of fear. I said goodnight and walked through the dark to a big ponderosa pine I'd laid my things beneath.

I had befriended several faculty members at the school, including the two English teachers. We talked about literature and writing instead of topographical maps and backpacking gear.

Almost ten years prior, when I was a sophomore in college, I was delighted to be admitted into a poetry writing workshop taught by Lucille Clifton. I wasn't an English major, but I loved her poems, especially this one:

> i am accused of tending to the past
> as if i made it,
> as if i sculpted it
> with my own hands. i did not.
> this past was waiting for me

when i came,
a monstrous unnamed baby,
and i with my mother's itch
took it to breast
and named it
History.
she is more human now,
learning languages every day,
remembering faces, names and dates.
when she is strong enough to travel
on her own, beware, she will.

I tried to emulate her work—writing short lines and short poems, using the small "i" the way she did. I knew I could not be like her, but I was adrift, casting about for voice, for self.

Lucille was both "Prof." and "prophet." I reserved a place in my class notebook to write down things she said, such as "Poems are very tricky because even if you don't take them seriously, they will take themselves seriously," and "One of the clichés about California is that in California everything is equal to everything else." She was oracular.

She wore black ballet slippers—real ones, the kind with a tiny swath of suede for a sole—as if she didn't need shoes the way the rest of us did and pirouetted from one segment of her day to the next rather than walk.

Two of her daughters lived with her, and they picked her up after class every week. They were a little older than me, both gorgeous with long black curls and deep brown skin. I ached with longing at their obvious resemblance to their mother and at her obvious adoration of them.

Lucille let me take her class three times in a row, as if she knew I needed to write my way through something and might do it if given the space.

———————

At the school in New Mexico, I told the English department chair, Hannah, about my interest in poetry, and she invited me to teach a creative writing unit in her class.

When I showed her the poems I had selected for her students to read and the writing prompts I'd developed to go with them, she said, "I didn't expect this level of sophistication from the wilderness teacher."

Her comment both stung and buoyed me, making me suspect that most of the faculty at the school considered me a dumb wilderness jock, but also boosting my confidence about teaching poetry.

After the first class, she called me into her office.

"Nice work," she said. "I think you should consider starting a weekly poetry workshop. I know of a few students who would like to continue working with you."

Sometimes my poetry students and I met in the tiny living room of my tiny A-frame cabin across the road from campus and drank hot cocoa while we wrote; sometimes we bundled in winter coats and hiked out to the sandstone canyon next to campus and sat in the dark under trees to write.

I loved teaching writing more than what I had been hired to teach—backcountry skiing technique and Wilderness First Aid.

I also wrote on my own, holed up in my cabin on long winter nights. When spring finally broke through the snow and ice, the other English teacher, Patty, and I wrote a comedy piece about ourselves and our shoes for a school event, and when we performed it, our students liked it so much, they asked us to reprise it at the year-end show.

Working at the international school made me want to go back to school. I was ready to emerge from the wilderness and I wanted to write about it, to start piecing together what all that wilderness travel had to do with my search for my birth parents.

Back in the Grand Canyon, I prepared to take six students down the Tanner Trail, a rugged, ten-mile route to the Colorado River. I had previously hiked it, so I knew to expect steep terrain with lots of boulder-hopping. My assistants were second-year students at the school: Jeanne, a practical and friendly girl from Indonesia, and Felipe, a skinny, long-haired guy from Colombia.

Everyone else was brand new to the school, to living in the United States, and to backpacking. Bibiana was a cute, petite girl from Guatemala; Daniel, a lanky bespectacled guy from Australia; Carla a hipster from Brazil; and Toshi was a prankstery, tall Japanese guy who pretended not to understand English when it benefited him.

After the lantern-lit talk from Kenneth, Toshi approached me as I shook out my sleeping bag in case snakes had crawled in while I was gone. "I liked what you said back there." He nodded his head as he struggled to find his words in English. "It was very brave of you to speak against Kenneth." He nodded again.

I set my bag down and looked up at him. "Thanks, I appreciate that." I wondered what he would be like as a hiking companion for the next few days.

We said goodnight, and he loped off on his long legs to his campsite. I slid into my bag underneath the tree to watch long bundles of pine needles puncture the starry sky. I was hoping for a feeling of connection with the universe, but instead I worried about having confronted Kenneth, and I worried about my health.

A rheumatologist had recently diagnosed my condition as Ankylosing Spondylitis, a chronic, inflammatory arthritis of the spine and sacroiliac joints. An autoimmune disorder, Ankylosing Spondylitis meant my immune system treated my connective tissue as foreign matter, attacking it as if it were a virus. Those attacks caused the inflammation and pain I'd been living with for eight years. The rheumatologist told me it would burden me for the rest of my life.

In many cases of the disease, vertebrae fuse together into something called bamboo spine. I looked it up in medical manuals and was alarmed to see pictures of patients permanently stuck in hunched positions. I tried to push these images out of my mind and keep my body moving, but the stress of knowing what could happen to me exacerbated my pain.

So did the exertion and lack of sleep from my work with New Mexico's

Search and Rescue team, a requirement of my job. I'd already been called out on several missions that required walking around all night at high elevation in search of lost hikers, only to have to report bright and early to work the next morning and lead a snow camping trip. I wasn't sure how long I'd be able to continue mustering the energy my job required.

Ankylosing Spondylitis is usually genetically inherited. Now that I had a definitive diagnosis, my desire to find my biological family only increased. If I found them, I might find out what to expect as my body aged.

In the morning, everyone readied to hike into the canyon. We drove to the trailhead, and my small hiking group filed out into the parking lot. Our bus snorted off as we walked, heavily, under loaded backpacks, to peer over the canyon's rim. The trail was a gully full of enormous boulders.

"Whoa," Toshi said.

Everyone laughed nervously.

We hoisted our packs, cinched our waist belts, and started picking our way down. Jeanne and I took the lead for the first part, and Felipe, looking a little bit like Kermit the Frog with his skinny legs sheathed in green long johns, offered to bring up the rear. The boulders were slick and difficult to balance on. It was slow going.

As a Grand Canyon ranger, I had learned that while hiking from rim to river, one moves through many plant and animal communities, or life zones, each with specific characteristics. Because of its extreme depth, the Grand Canyon includes more life zones than almost any place on earth. The rim, at 7,000 feet, is a cold climate forest, and below it live the animals and plants of the high desert, then the low desert. The river hosts yet another zone—of riparian plants and animals.

Hiking down is like descending a staircase with many landings. But these "landings" aren't discrete. Early twentieth-century philosopher-scientist Aldo Leopold noticed transitional zones between them, which he called edges. He found species living at the intersection between zones which were uniquely adapted to both. Biologists call them "edge species."

During the first hours of our hike through some of those overlapping zones, I began to experience the sense of being home, of being absorbed by the landscape. It was That Expansive Canyon Feeling.

I delighted in looking at the sandstone and limestone buttes I had climbed, whose names I knew: Zoroaster, Shiva, Brahma, Vishnu. Long ago, someone named them after gods and called them temples.

By midday we were halfway to the river, well into the low desert zone, and completely exposed on the Tonto Plateau. I suggested a sunscreen break.

Toshi stopped in the middle of the trail and squeezed a glob of white goo into his hand. "How much longer until we get to the bottom?"

"A couple hours." I said.

A few of them sighed. We moved on, now with me in the lead and Jeanne in the back, on the circuitous route around Escalante and Cardenas Buttes, which looked like giant red bat wings in the distance. The route through the Redwall Limestone cliffs was steep and had lots of scree on the trail that made us slip, as if we were trying to walk on little ball bearings. But we were rewarded with panoramic views of canyon after canyon inside the mother of all canyons.

Finally, we found the wide wash near the river, and everyone was relieved to be done hiking. Jeanne found a spot for our camp kitchen in a thicket of feathery-leaved tamarisk trees with a clearing in the middle. The wash was scattered with large, river-smoothed stones of many colors. They were lovely, but held little promise for comfortable sleeping.

We made a dinner of fajitas with beans and cheese, bell peppers and onions. Sautéing the vegetables made me think of how I had learned to cook.

My parents were both busy working people with little time to devote to meal preparation and even less interest in the culinary world. When I was twelve, and my brothers were nine and ten, my parents decided that we were all old enough to be given the responsibility of making dinner for the whole family one night per week.

I was incensed. None of my friends had to make dinner for their family. I wondered why I should have to. I wanted to be taken care of. This development in the cooperative experiment that was my family did not fall into my definition of nurturance.

To this day, I don't really understand what my parents thought we would cook. My Midwestern parents made a lot of dinners using cans of cream of mushroom soup: Tuna Noodle Casserole, Hamburger Casserole, and something called "Hot Tamale Pie."

Each of us kids developed our own approach to assigned dinner nights. Since I was fervently opposed to the idea, I protested by heating canned chicken noodle soup every Tuesday evening. Sometimes I cut up pieces of Monterey Jack cheese and threw it in the soup for extra flavor, and other times I included a side of sliced French bread, but that was the extent of the variation in my cooking regimen. I did that for six years.

My youngest brother Jason, a mere nine years old when Dinner Night took effect, was a budding pyromaniac, so every Friday night until I graduated from high school we ate hot dogs he'd torched on the tiny hibachi grill on our back porch.

At age ten, my brother Brian was interested in cooking, and he spent all his free time volunteering behind the counter at the charcuterie shop in our little town. He was the only kid I've ever known who possessed a Cuisinart food processor and a subscription to *Cook's Magazine*. He learned much from the charcuterie shop's owners and was happy to have the opportunity to try out his culinary fantasies on us at home. Unfortunately, while he was the most enthusiastic cook among the five of us, he was not the most detail-oriented, so some of his concoctions were only borderline edible, but they were no worse than my offerings of canned soup or Jason's burned hot dogs. And the first time I ever ate tofu, my ten-year-old brother cooked it for me, sautéed with onions and bell peppers.

Although my parents never complained about the food we cooked, I can't imagine they enjoyed eating it. Perhaps they figured it was better than having to cook for all of us every night. Yet they never sat down with us and opened a cookbook or discussed meal planning ideas. I am still unclear about whether they were rabidly anti-cookbook or just really didn't mind eating high sodium, highly processed, and burned foods. Or whether they thought their experiment in family participation was more valuable than nutrition.

We all grew to normal sizes with normal IQs, so the poor eating didn't seem to harm us. but the Dinner Night arrangement gave me another opportunity to feel adrift. For years, we kids had been expected to get ourselves up and out of bed in the morning, make our own breakfasts, pack our school lunches, and ride our bikes to and from school, all without adult supervision. And now dinner. What did family mean, I wondered, if you had to do all these things for yourself by the time you were twelve years old? I'd pedal to school on my sparkly green bike, feeling that no one was watching out for me.

Of course, I knew this wasn't exactly true: my parents did take care of us. They came home every evening, hugged us and told us they loved us, made sure we did our homework, signed us up for sports and theater classes. They sat with us at dinner and listened to our stories and laughed at our jokes.

But their interest in providing us freedoms that they hadn't been afforded in their own childhoods was misspent on me, a girl who just wanted to feel wanted. I had lost one set of parents when I was born. My parents gave me so much autonomy that I ended up feeling like I had lost them too.

My brothers, only fifteen months apart in age, had each other. As little kids, they made elaborate spaceship command centers out of our wooden toy blocks, laying them out in geometric patterns across the living room floor and sneaking felt-tipped markers to draw colorful buttons and switches on them. They sat together in the middle of their flight deck and flew their spaceship around, yelling commands to each other, Captain Kirk and Spock on the Starship *Enterprise*. Or Han Solo and Chewbacca on the *Millennium Falcon*.

I had no interest in playing with blocks or pretending to be in outer space. I squeezed into a niche of my own in a bookshelf and held my doll while I sucked my thumb and watched my brothers in their imaginary world. They were in outer space; I was trying to draw myself closer to the earth—I didn't want to feel like a floating space baby.

Jason was born to my parents, but like me, Brian was adopted. Also like mine, Brian's was a closed adoption, so he had scant information about his birth parents.

When I first got my non-identifying information, I asked Brian if he had considered trying to find his birth parents.

"Why would I do that?" he asked. "They obviously don't want to know me."

I understood that feeling. There was a lot to lose. We were both scared of being rejected twice by our biological parents. That was the only time Brian ever said anything about it to me. We were siblings, but we had different needs regarding connection to the past.

By the time my group of students and I finished dinner and scrubbed the dishes in Colorado River water, it was late and everyone was exhausted. We all wandered off to nooks between cobbles where we had settled our sleeping bags for the night.

I awoke at dawn with the feeling of someone watching me. Opening my eyes, I saw my assistant Felipe's face only a foot away from mine.

"Andrea," he whispered, crouching among the cobbles, his brown eyes mischievous. "Do you think we could mix some hot cocoa powder with onions and bell peppers and pancake batter for breakfast this morning?"

I laughed. The breakfast idea sounded truly disgusting. Soon we were both cracking up, our laughter echoing like raven calls across the river stones in the predawn glow. Felipe bounded over to our camp kitchen to make the pancakes that sounded so unappetizing.

It was a layover day, which we spent exploring our surroundings. Toshi found a huge area of quicksand near the river and called everyone over. Soon, we were all playing in quicksand. If we kept our legs moving fast enough, we didn't sink into it, and it made a trampoliney kind of bounce. Water filled the holes where our feet had been.

Toshi stood about twenty feet away from me, up to his knees in quicksand. "Pull your feet out before you sink more!" I called over Tanner Rapids' roar.

He pretended not to understand me and stood smiling, sinking a little deeper.

"Really, don't sink any deeper."

Toshi still didn't move. I pulled out my own feet and started trampolining my way over to him. Toshi began straining to extract his right foot. It didn't budge. Just as I reached him, his leg emerged with a thick, wet smack. Parts of his sandal hung like ribbons from his ankle, the rest buried in the sticky quicksand.

He yelped, surprised, and pulled out his other foot. Same thing: ribbons of sandal. He lay down on his belly and began digging like a dog for the soles of his shoes. I couldn't believe what I was watching.

"Get up! Your sandals aren't worth saving," I said. "Get out of the quicksand."

He kept digging. Eventually he stood, holding one sole in each hand. "Got them!" he cried, a goofy smile on his face. We made our way to dry sand, and he began trying to repair his footwear.

"Don't go deeper than your ankles anymore," I told everyone. We were all duly cowed by watching Toshi's struggle.

We went back to playing more safely near the edge of the quicksand, bouncing around in a big circle. Felipe hung back, pointing his camera at our feet, clicking off shots of sunlight and water as they filled the apertures of our steps, of legs straining against the pull of strange stuff that was not quite liquid, not quite solid—something in between, unnamable, dangerous, and unknowable.

Before he graduated that spring, Felipe held a photography exhibition in the art building at school. I found myself standing in front of an image of Toshi's and my legs dancing in quicksand, the other students dancing in the background, the Colorado River rushing behind us. The glossy wet surface we trod upon bent beneath our weight, but it did not break.

Chapter 11

Participate in Your Own Rescue

(On the Colorado River through the Grand Canyon)

You can't revenge yourself against Mother Nature.

—Patti Smith

The only legal search method available to adoptees born in Colorado was the Confidential Intermediary Program, created to allow adoptees to hire a state-appointed searcher who would have access to sealed records and classified search tools to find "the sought-after" person. According to the program's guidelines, the intermediary would locate my birth mother, contact her, and tell her that I was looking for her. At that point, my birth mother could refuse or accept contact. If she refused, any information the searcher had found would be sealed and, by law, never reopened, and I would have no legal right to any of it. I would never know my birth mother's name or anything about her.

But if my birth mother accepted, the intermediary would obtain court-approved permission from both of us to disclose contact information to each other, and we would reunite in a manner of our choosing.

I could only focus on the former outcome: that my birth mother would reject me. I couldn't imagine that she would say, "Yes, I want to be found," to a faceless intermediary stranger who phoned to ask if she was my biological mother. The way I saw it, it would be very easy to refuse and hang up. Forever. And then it would be over, the records re-sealed, and I would be worse off than I had been before.

I couldn't bear the thought that she might be found and I would still be denied access to her. For several years I had sporadically entertained, and then struck down, the idea of applying to the intermediary program. I felt as powerless as a child—to the rules of the intermediary process and the whims of my birth mother. I hated having so little control over information I truly felt was mine.

I decided I'd try to find her myself. After a year at the international school, I quit. My only plan was to search.

I had ten days of rafting on the Colorado River with some friends to think through how to do it. Getting ready for the raft trip, I packed up my belongings in my A-frame cabin and came across the files of my non-identifying information and notes from Lorraine, the ALMA volunteer. I wrote a list of her ideas for pursuing my search: visiting the genealogy departments of public libraries in small towns in Colorado and the archives at the university I thought my birth mother had attended, and looking at old phone books for listings of irrigation supply businesses that might have belonged to my paternal grandfather.

I felt a need to go to Colorado to acquaint myself with the landscape, my original one. I would drive to Colorado after the rafting trip. Perhaps it would be like navigating wilderness. I could find my bearings using the Rocky Mountains and the Great Plains as handrails and follow the contour lines of the Front Range's foothills the same way I had used topographic maps to find my way while hiking.

I would travel through the patchworked farm country north of Boulder where I thought my birth parents had lived, drive the right-angled rural roads cornering farms and ranches. Motoring around looking for clues would be taking on a new kind of wilderness.

On the first day of the river trip, I fell in love with the canyon in a new way: all the side canyons our boats rocked past became metaphors for my search. Each canyon seemed like a door that might lead to discovery, an insight furthering my search. But also on that first day, my love for the canyon was tested.

Before sunrise, I had hit the trail into the canyon to join ten friends from my hometown who had begun their trip seven days and ninety-five miles upriver at Lees Ferry, a boat launch downstream of the Glen Canyon Dam.

To me, the dam seemed like its own kind of closed adoption, creating a blockade that changed the environment of animals and plants above and below it. Separating them from each other.

The dam also wrought changes on the river's sediment levels, temperature, and volume. It eroded beach sand that would never redeposit. It endangered native fish by obliterating their habitat.

And the reservoir behind the dam, Lake Powell, drowned canyons, inundating countless archaeological sites, whole villages gone forever.

The dam had stolen huge chunks of history, obviously a sensitive spot for me.

When I arrived at the river, my friends gave me some tips about how to run Grand Canyon rapids: if I fell out of the boat or the boat flipped over, I should point my feet downstream so I could kick away from rocks and try to swim across the current to the shore.

With that, I hopped into a large inflatable oar raft, and Suzanne, an oarswoman whom I'd just met, rowed us out into the current. I wasn't fearful, but only because I didn't know what lay ahead. I felt confident I could follow the instructions for handling a boat flip, but I was pretty sure it wouldn't happen. I had never been knocked out of a raft before. Why would it happen now?

Suzanne, red-haired and four months pregnant, sat on a huge cooler full of food for the ten-day trip. Her small baby bump protruded from beneath her shirt as she yanked on the oars. She had been testing herself against the rapids since the launch at Lees Ferry. I was in awe of her super-toughness, rowing through the Grand Canyon while pregnant. I liked her right away.

Sitting on one of the raft's air-filled tubes, I chatted with her as she rowed through some flat water. "How has the trip been for you so far?" I nodded at her bump.

"It's been harder than I thought," she said, looking at the water to make sure her line through the current was correct. "I get tired a lot more easily than I thought I would. And I keep fantasizing about eating Pringles potato chips. It's all I can think about."

There were probably few places in the United States where we had a slimmer chance of getting our hands on a can of Pringles than the bottom of the Grand Canyon.

"I wish I could help you with that," I said. "If I'd known, I would have been happy to shove a few cans in my pack before I hiked down here."

"I've got a plan to throw myself at the mercy of the next commercial river boat trip we float by. 'Pringles for the Pregnant' is a catchy plea, right?"

I laughed, liking her even more. And the fact that she was about to become a mother felt like kismet.

The tricky part about starting a raft trip through the Grand Canyon at the halfway point instead of at Lees Ferry is that passengers have little time to get their river legs under them before entering some of the canyon's biggest rapids, which are also some of the world's biggest rapids.

Suzanne and I glided up to Hermit Rapid, one of the canyon's biggest.

Back when I lived on the rim, I had hiked the Hermit Trail down to this rapid, companioned by petrified claw tracks left by ancient reptiles hiking across prehistoric sand dunes, now solid rock.

Suzanne eddied out, parking the boat above the rapid to scout it and determine the safest route to row through it.

I stood on the shore's wet sand with the bowline and bail bucket in hand, watching the rapid's huge undulations. Hermit Rapid is a sequence of several giant, hunchbacked waves running down the middle of the channel.

Suzanne found a line she wanted to take, and we hopped back in our boat. She pulled hard on the oars to position the boat correctly to ride the wave train. I held the bail bucket at the ready.

As we gained the crest of the very first wave, the boat flipped backward. I was thrown into bristling cold water. The current grabbed my limbs and agitated me into the second wave as if I were a dirty shirt in need of washing. The trough of that wave sucked me under. I held my breath as long as I could, hoping the river would release me before I ran out of air.

Finally, my head popped up and I gasped for air like a newborn as the river carried me up and over the wave, then dropped me into the next trough. This happened five more times, each time the current pulling me deeper. I thought my lungs would explode before the river released me to the air, but each time the river freed me just before that happened.

I pushed my head out of the freezing water a final time and paddled out of the rapid's aftermath toward the nearest shore, fighting the bulk of the orange life jacket that had kept me from drowning.

"Participate in your own rescue!" someone yelled.

I didn't understand, kept paddling toward shore.

"Participate in your own rescue!" someone yelled again.

I looked up, numbly, still swimming, to see a muscled woman wearing a long-billed cap standing on the edge of our overturned raft, holding a rope she'd rigged to right the boat. She dangled it near me.

I recognized her as one of a group of women kayakers we'd seen who were making their way through the canyon on the same schedule as our group. They had stopped to help when they saw us flip.

I flopped onto a boulder in the shallows, attempting to get out of the river and help her right the boat, to do what I had been told: participate in my own rescue. But I shook uncontrollably from the chill of the forty-degree water and the sheer terror of nearly drowning seven times.

Cory, an oarsman in my group saw me wobbling toward the rope and grabbed me before I fell, leaving the muscled woman to right the boat herself. I sat on the boulder shivering, arms wrapped around my knees, teeth chattering from cold and residual adrenaline, and feeling like a total loser. Pregnant Suzanne sat on the shore not far from me, also shaken but unharmed.

Had I failed my beloved canyon or had it failed me? My love affair with it was about five years old by then, and although I had hiked and explored many miles of it on foot, I had mostly stayed a respectful distance from the river itself. I loved to swim, and I'd jump into almost any water, but the immense power of the Colorado River had always scared me off. It was hard to find a place to wade in deeper than shin-level without the current sweeping me away, without getting my breath stolen by its cold.

Days before I drove to the rim, I had called Lutheran Social Services, the agency in Denver that handled my adoption, and made an appointment to meet with Danielle, the social worker who had sent me my non-identifying information.

Our meeting was scheduled to take place a few days after my river trip ended. I wondered about Danielle. Would she be grandmotherly? Sympathetic to my cause? Or was she a rule follower who would merely reiterate the ambiguous information she'd already given me to keep me from what I wanted?

In anticipation of my search trip to Colorado, I'd talked to my mom about where my birth mother might have gone to school.

"The teacher's college was in Greeley," she said. "That's where young women went to school in those days if they wanted to become teachers."

The town of Greeley would be a main locus of my search. But had my birth mother grown up in Greeley or just attended college there? I didn't know if there was any way to determine that.

I felt guilty about it, but I switched out of Suzanne's boat after Hermit into a boat with Cory, an expert boatman and blacksmith who hammered the intricate iron gates of opulent vacation homes in Aspen, Colorado. His arms looked as if he had forged them, too, of iron.

One night, as our whole group lay on sleeping mats on white sand, looking up at the glut of stars above the rim, I reached over to Cory's hand and intertwined my fingers with his. He slid his blacksmith's arm under my head and I slept on it that night and every night thereafter on the trip.

The simple fact that Cory lived in Colorado drew me to him. I imagined moving to Colorado to look for my birth parents. Perhaps I'd move near him; perhaps he would help me with my search. Maybe I wouldn't have to do it alone.

In a history book I brought on the trip, I read that in 1928, newlyweds Glen and Bessie Hyde set out to raft the Grand Canyon: Bessie wanted to be the first woman in recorded history to complete the trip. But she and her new husband never returned, and their boat was found empty in an eddy deep in the canyon. They were never heard from again.

Bessie hadn't just bailed water like me—she captained. I scrutinized pictures of her standing on their wooden raft, using a pole to guide it. I imagined her developing muscular arms like the woman who had righted my raft in Hermit Rapid.

What happened to Bessie and her beloved? Their bodies were never recovered, and some people speculated they stole off to Mexico to start anew, but most figured they drowned.

I liked imagining that they lived on, hidden deep in a remote corner of the canyon, their honeymoon world. That maybe someday they could be found.

During stretches of calm water I sat in the boat, life vest tightly fastened across my chest as the multihued layers of the canyon shifted by. I watched the faraway blue sky framed by the canyon's rims, listening to the silence that abounds below.

My search plan bobbed alongside me constantly like an errant paddle, my loneliness amplified by the fact that although Cory let me sleep on his arm all night and kissed me tenderly in the darkness of the canyon's shadows, during the days he all but ignored me, focusing instead on the lines of rapids, rowing through them perfectly as I frantically bailed buckets of river water from his boat.

There's something to be said for being prepared for what you take on. As the days drifted by, I watched the group of kayaking women who had rescued us maneuvering gleefully through rapids, then dragging their boats back up to the tongue of whitewater and dropping into them again and again, whooping the whole time.

I didn't know if I was prepared to search or not. I had waited a long time to move forward with it. Was I ready to meet the challenge? I didn't expect to experience the search as a rapid I wanted to run again and again, but I gained some insight from the trip about wildness and limitation, about tugging on a line to right a boat and peering inside to see what might still be there. Or what might be swirling down to the river bottom with Bessie and Glen Hyde.

Chapter 12

Empty Shoes

(On the Road through Arizona, Colorado, Utah, and Nevada)

Ascetic and maternal, you endure…
With your mute patience.

—Charles Simic

At the takeout, Cory and I deflated and rolled his raft into a giant white burrito in the dusty heat at the river's edge. We drove to Flagstaff to return the rafting gear to a warehouse.

"Do you want to go into town and find a motel together for the night?" he asked. Though I hoped for a hint of lust or desire in his voice, his tone remained matter-of-fact, his intentions inscrutable as ever.

My mouth dropped open a little, and I tried to conceal my surprise at his offer. But I was up for more adventure, whatever that meant. Maybe he would finally make a move on me.

"Sure," I said, feeling a little giddy. I smiled at his sunburned face, his deeply freckled Irish skin and red hair bleached almost white from the canyon sun.

Finishing at the warehouse, we hugged everyone good-bye and drove into town. Because I was curious to see what he would do, I asked Cory to choose our lodging. Neither of us had showered in weeks, so any motel would have been clean compared to our bodies. Except the one he chose.

We waited on the lobby's shabby couch while a maid attended to the room we were to occupy. I watched cars on the freeway reel past the window, feeling the peculiar hum my body generated whenever I emerged from wilderness into the world of roads and vehicles and speed and couches and beds. It was a pleasant buzz shot through with loss, a bittersweet letting go of the ecstatic.

———————————

A black velvet picture of a wildcat hung above the bed. The toilet sported one of those paper strips proclaiming it had been "Sanitized!" yet the bowl was woefully unflushed. I laughed, partly out of disbelief, and partly because it was a strangely perfect finish to the trip. Still chuckling, I pushed the toilet handle and hoped the contents would disappear, then jumped in the shower and did my best to scrub all the sand off my body.

When I emerged somewhat desanded, Cory asked, "Are there enough towels in the bathroom?"

"Lots," I said, wrapping one around my head. "Why?"

"The maid just called to tell us they're going to bring us more towels."

"Weird," I said, knitting my brows. "That's more service than I would expect at this place, given the state of the room." I picked a long black hair from a pillow and held it up as evidence.

We both laughed, bodies quaking, loopy from the exhaustion that sets in once a long trip in the backcountry ends.

"I'll call them back and tell them we don't need any towels," he said. But just as he picked up the phone, someone knocked on the door.

"Housekeeping. Towels," said a cheery male voice behind the door.

Cory opened the door, and something white flew past him into the room. He jumped back. Another something white flew in. And another. Standard issue motel towels continued sailing in through the door, landing limply all over the room. I stood frozen in place.

"Surprise!" yelled Suzanne and her husband, Will, walking through the door. Their arms were laden with yet more towels.

Still too stunned to speak, I picked up a towel and swatted at Suzanne with it.

"I thought you'd already left for Albuquerque!" Cory said.

I picked up another towel and threw it at Will.

He batted the towel away. "We saw you parking your car at this place and decided to stay the night and see if you wanted to go out to dinner with us."

Suzanne sat heavily on the saggy bed, her pregnant belly now prominent. She looked around the dingy room. "Nice choice of digs, folks."

I sat down next to her and gave her a side-hug. "Let's get out of here and find some Thai food," I said.

———————

We ate curry and drank lots of Singha beer. Suzanne and Will, always up for more fun, suggested we go out dancing at a local nightclub.

Cory demurred. "I've got a long drive home tomorrow. You all have a good time. I'm going back to our fancy motel."

I took that as an indication that he was not up for fun of any kind. A night of dancing with people I liked sounded like a perfect way to extend the wildness of the river trip just a little longer, to pay it homage and put it to bed, so I gave up on Cory and headed out with Will and Suzanne.

At two in the morning, sweaty from dancing, stinking of beer, and still itchy from sand, I slid into the bed next to Cory, who was fast asleep.

———————

At first light, I packed up my dusty hatchback, hugged Cory good-bye, and began the six-hundred-mile drive to Boulder, Colorado, where my friend Alice lived. She had offered me her apartment while she was away on vacation. I appreciated her generosity, but I wished she were home so that I would have someone to talk to about my search, someone to drink a glass of wine with at the end of the day while I described my plan to sneak around the Front Range trying to find clues to my past. Instead, I found her cozy room with a futon on the floor and too much solitude.

I awoke, head spinning with who and where my birth parents might be. Brushing my teeth, I looked at myself in Alice's bathroom mirror. The crow's feet around my eyes had deepened during my year in New Mexico's backcountry. I was twenty-nine years old but didn't feel like an adult. I was still a baby who had been given away. Did I expect finding my birth parents would solve all my problems, clarify who I was and what I should do with my life? I was looking for big answers, pinning hopes for direction in life on those shadow people. Desperation swirled around me, a self-inflicted storm. Would I really feel better once I knew who they were?

———————

I readied myself for my appointment with Danielle, the social worker at the agency. Adoption rights advocates I'd talked with had told me that social workers who were sympathetic to adoptees in search would sometimes meet with them in their offices, then excuse themselves from the room after chatting a bit, leaving a piece of paper on the desk that had a scrap of identifying information on it: a birth parent's name, for instance. Of course, I wanted Danielle to be this kind of social worker. But I also had a backup plan to ask a series of questions based on my non-identifying information in hopes that she would slip up and tell me something.

———————

Making my way to the office of Lutheran Social Services in Denver to meet her, I realized that after a year of driving gravel roads in the tiny town where I'd lived in northern New Mexico, Denver's traffic and dense population felt too fast and noisy. And even though the information I sought was rightfully mine, I felt as if I were doing something illicit. My hands gripped the steering wheel more tightly than usual.

———————

Air conditioning slapped me when I walked into the building. In the lobby, Danielle approached me. She was a tall woman in her sixties, with short white hair and a gentle smile.

"Let's show you around the office," she said.

I bit at my lips. I didn't care what the office looked like. But maybe she thought I would envision it as a kind of home since my birth mother had once entered the building, because the names of my birth mother and birth father were written on a slip of paper in a file somewhere within.

When I thought about it though, it did feel onerous to stand in the building that held definitive information about my origins. I walked alongside Danielle, trying to be polite, nodding, smiling, and shaking hands with other social workers, but distracted by my fantasy of tearing around rooms, ripping open file cabinets, grabbing documents, and shoving rolls of microfiche under my shirt.

After the tour, Danielle suggested we go somewhere for lunch. My heart raced. I was positive she was communicating to me in code that she couldn't talk about my case while we were in the office, but if we left the building she would be able to give me the information I sought. She asked me to wait in her office while she collected her things to leave.

This might be my chance: vacating the office might be her invitation to look around the room for information. I walked in, trembling a bit, hoping, and half expecting, to see a file folder with my name penned in red lying on the Formica desktop.

The desk was completely bare, computer turned off, file cabinet closed. My shoulders slumped. As I tried to muster the nerve to jiggle its handle to see if it was locked, Danielle returned. My body pulsed with disappointment and fear that I wouldn't get any new information from the visit.

We walked out into the August noon to a little Mexican restaurant in a strip mall. I was sweating when we arrived. The restaurant was cool and cavernous inside, and it felt like a good place for a secret meeting. A jolt of hope shot through my belly. Danielle asked me where I had grown up. I twisted my napkin under the table. "We moved to northern California when I turned one. My dad got a job as a professor there," I said.

Danielle sipped her water out of its plastic cup. "And where do you live now?" she asked.

I don't live anywhere, I thought. But I said, "I've been living in New Mexico, working as a wilderness guide at a small college. I just got off a rafting trip through the Grand Canyon." I smiled weakly, thinking of the canyon and how lonely and forsaken I'd felt on the trip.

"I've heard boating the canyon is a wonderful experience," Danielle replied, smiling.

"Yes, it was like nothing I've ever done before." I recalled the flipped boat in Hermit Rapid, the nights spent with my head resting on Cory's arm, the daydreaming I'd done about this very moment with Danielle.

The waitress arrived with my plate of enchiladas and Danielle's burrito and set them on the table. I cut a gooey piece.

"How long have you been working with Lutheran Social Services?" I twisted my napkin again.

"Thirty-five years, if you can believe it."

My eyes widened. "You were there when I was born?"

"Yes, I was."

My heart beat rapidly. Had she seen me when I was an infant? Had she interviewed my birth mother when she placed me for adoption?

"I'm sorry, I was not the social worker assigned to your case. She retired years ago."

My heart felt like it was shrinking. Danielle had anticipated my next question and shut it down. Still, I wondered if she had seen me as a days-old baby going into foster care or as a three-week-old baby being adopted by my parents, if she had held me, or had at least cooed at me while I was bundled up asleep in someone's arms in the agency's waiting room.

And if she hadn't, who had held me, fed me, and dressed me when I was a newborn? I felt like I was going to explode. I had no answers to any of my questions, and I had no legal right to those answers. Sitting there in the stupid strip mall restaurant, I wanted to tear the neon beer sign off the wall and smash it.

Palms sweating, I grabbed my fork to cut another chunk of enchilada, but the fork slipped out of my hand, clattering to the tile floor below the table. Danielle looked up at me, startled.

I smiled weakly, took a quick breath. "You may have guessed that I've decided to try to search for my birth mother." I flagged down the waitress to ask for a new fork. "I have a letter signed by my adoptive parents stating their support for my search and asking the agency to help me." I located the dropped fork with my foot and stepped on it, flattening its tines just to feel them bend.

Danielle dabbed the corners of her mouth with her napkin. "Yes, I assumed you were here because you want to search. I'm glad your parents are sympathetic to your wishes." She gave a too-quick smile.

I kept my foot on the fork. "I also have a letter stating that I give permission for the agency to give my birth parents my contact information if they're looking for me. Would you put it in my file?"

Danielle agreed to do it.

I took a deep breath and asked, "Has your agency received any word from my birth mother or birth father since my adoption, asking for information about me or providing information about themselves?" I held my breath, as if it would skew the answer in my favor.

Danielle's eyes crinkled a little at the edges. She spoke in a soft voice. "I checked your file before you arrived, and there was nothing like that. I'm sorry."

My chest tightened. No one was looking for me. In twenty-nine years, no one had even tried, hadn't made the small gesture of sending a letter to the agency. It wasn't a complete surprise: a few years earlier, when I put my name on several adoption registries, the databases and forums that list an adoptee's or a birth parent's contact information and details about who they're searching for, I had found no matches, so I already suspected no one was actively looking for me. Still, hearing it aloud from Danielle made it definitive.

I wondered if my birth parents were dead or in denial of my existence. Maybe they didn't feel they had the right to search for me. My mouth went dry. "Is there anything you can tell me to help me with my search?" I asked.

Danielle folded her paper napkin and placed it on the table. "Since your adoption is a closed one, I'm not at liberty to reveal information that would identify your birth parents," she said, her voice still soft.

Apparently, our trip to the Mexican restaurant was not a clandestine meeting—it was just lunch. I stopped eating. The cheese in my enchiladas congealed while a voice in my head said *This is your information! She won't give it to you if you don't ask for it. No one else is going to do this for you.*

It was difficult to embody the confidence to ask her questions she might refuse to answer. Part of me still felt like an abandoned child who should avoid rocking the boat, should be grateful for being adopted at all.

But I took another deep breath and asked her, "Since both of my birth mother's parents were Norwegian, did she have a Scandinavian-sounding last name?" I cringed a little.

"I suppose you could say that," she replied.

I felt my cheeks flush. I had scored a point, albeit a vague one. "I also read that she wanted to go to school to be a teacher." I held eye contact with Danielle. "The local teacher's college was the Colorado State University at Greeley: is that where she was enrolled when she became pregnant?"

She looked me right in the eye. "Yes, that's where she was."

I sat up a bit taller in the booth—at last, I had one solid piece of information. I had one more question. I hesitated, jiggled my leg. "Which letter of the alphabet does my birth mother's surname begin with?" The fork slipped from under my foot and clanged against a table leg.

Danielle grew still. "I can't give you that kind of information."

Face red, heart beating fast, I took a sip of my Diet Coke, trying to wash away the feelings of embarrassment and anger. What could I ask now? Nothing.

But in the over-air-conditioned darkness of the restaurant, an idea occurred to me. Now that I knew my birth mother had attended Greeley, perhaps I could obtain the college's enrollment records from the fall semester of 1966 and compare the names of newly enrolled women with those still enrolled in spring 1967. Then I would be able to make a list of all the first-year women who had been there in the fall but hadn't returned for the spring term.

My birth mother would be on that list.

It was my first breakthrough. It seemed like an elegant plan; since Danielle had said it was a Scandinavian name, I could find the ones that sounded Scandinavian, then track down those women. There would only be a few names, maybe ten or twenty. Perhaps Danielle had given me enough information to progress in my search.

"I understand," I said, my breath coming a little easier. "Thank you so much for your time."

She patted my hand. "Good luck with your search," she said. We settled the bill and walked in awkward silence back to the adoption agency.

I drove through the Front Range's bright pasturelands to Greeley, a town smelling of cattle feedlots, and found the university library. The archives were in the basement, a small room with a few tables, people sitting at some of them.

I approached the information counter and requested copies of enrollment records for fall of 1966 and spring of 1967. I stood waiting for them to photocopy the documents I needed, jiggling my leg. After a while, the woman working behind the counter emerged and handed me two heavy stacks of warm paper. I ran my trembling hands over them, then sat down to begin the work of comparing semesters, highlighting in yellow the names of young women who might be my birth mother.

After the first three pages, I looked up and gave my head a quick shake. There were not going to be just ten or twenty names. I was highlighting several per page. What had happened to all of those girls who disappeared between fall and spring?

I continued highlighting missing girls for over an hour. There were more than two hundred first-year girls enrolled in the fall of 1966 who had disappeared from school by the spring of 1967. I scanned the list of names, pressed my hands to my temples. Many names looked Scandinavian.

My disappointment must have been obvious because a middle-aged woman with dark hair sitting at a nearby table discreetly handed me an index card. I took it from her and read "I have heard there are only six degrees of separation between any two people on earth. Maybe I can help you find who you're looking for. Please email me if you'd like my assistance." There was a name, Maureen, and an email address at the bottom of the card.

I jerked my head back to see her and found that she had left the room. My whole body began to tingle. Was Maureen my birth mother? Why had she walked out so quickly? I gathered my things and ran out of the archive room to find her, searching hallways, bookstacks, bathrooms, but she wasn't anywhere. I ran into the library's computer lab and tapped out an email to her at the address she'd given me:

Dear Maureen,

Thanks so much for reaching out to me. I am un-
dergoing a very lonely and scary process: I'm
looking for my birth mother who attended college
here in 1966. I was born in May 1967 and placed
for adoption. I have obtained some information
about her family: both of her parents were Norwegian, and her family lived somewhere nearby
in Colorado. I only know a few things about her:
she was on a swim team in high school, and she
was an only child. When you saw me in the archives, I was making a list of female first-year
students who attended at Greeley in the fall of
1966, but who were no longer enrolled in the
spring. My birth mother should be one of the
names on this list.

Unfortunately, there are at least two hundred
names. I am a little stumped about what to do.
If you have any leads, I would be truly grateful
for your help.

Thanks again,
Andrea

I sat in the computer lab, checking every minute or so to see if she'd
returned my message, but there was nothing from her. In the late afternoon, I slumped to my car and drove back to Boulder.

In a restaurant above a little bookstore, I set the giant stack of paper
on the table and ordered a glass of white wine. When it arrived, I took a
big slug of it and set it atop the stack. I watched condensation from its
base soaking into the paper, penetrating the list in a way I couldn't.

The next morning, I checked my email and found this waiting for me:

Dear Andrea,

I was touched to see you searching in the university's library. I went to college there, and
I had an abortion in '68. I have always wondered
what would have happened if I had made a different choice. Had my choice been adoption, I would
very much want to know my child. Helping you is
a compensatory measure. I would be delighted
if you were mine, but I was not subject to the
emotional trauma that your birth mother experienced. I know you realize that upon finding her
you may be rejected. I would hate to see you
hurt, but I would also hate for you to miss the
opportunity for a connection with your birth
mother. I have some information that might help
you. I went to Valley High School in Gilcrest,
Colorado, and the school had a swimming pool.
I'm not sure if it had a team, but I could try
to find a yearbook to compare it to your list of
girls who dropped out of Greeley.

Best Wishes,
Maureen

Maureen was not my birth mother, nor did she know who my birth
mother was; Maureen was a grieving woman who had made a difficult
decision when she was very young. And she saw in me the specter of her
lost child. Her loss and mine were twinned. Despite the sadness of Maureen's story, I felt bolstered by her support. I finally felt like I had someone
on my side.

I spent the rest of the week at municipal libraries looking at high school
yearbooks for evidence of swim teams and Norwegian surnames, driving

around farm communities and stopping into irrigation supply stores to ask men who looked to be about my paternal grandfather's age if they knew of the family I was looking for. But I didn't make any headway, and it was time for me to leave Colorado. I had budgeted my savings to last until the end of summer, and it was mid-August. The vast expanses of eastern Colorado, Utah, and Nevada lay between my hometown destination and me. I had a lot of solo miles to roll across in my non-air-conditioned car during the next week or two.

———————

I road-tripped with the list of two hundred young women's names propped up on my passenger seat like a traveling companion, and the first night, I stopped to camp at Great Sand Dunes National Park. Sitting alone by a fire I built—not for warmth but to keep myself company—I began knitting a hat for a friend who was due to have a baby soon and thought about Maureen's pregnancy and my birth mother's as I formed the yarn into the shape of a baby's head.

I'd talked to almost no one for days, as if I'd taken a vow to speak only when necessary to make sacred, or at least make sense of, my search attempt in Colorado. I probably would have rambled on if I had spoken with anyone.

I awoke at dawn, before anyone else in the campground stirred, and hiked to the tallest dune, ascending it, then rolling down, somersaulting for what felt like miles. I found a blanched joy in it: the tumbling made me light-headed and shaky, just like everything else I was trying to do.

———————

A few days later, driving Highway 50 through Nevada, a span of interstate dubbed The Loneliest Highway in America, I listened to hours of AM talk radio for lack of any other choices in that vast unpopulated area. Hapless women phoned a psychology "expert" for advice about their struggles with romantic love as single parents.

She exhorted them, "Put your child first. Be your child's mother." Irony crackled in my brain.

It grew hotter and hotter inside my car, but there was nowhere to stop and cool off. I drove on, chugging water, the "expert" advice rattling in my head: "Be your child's mother. Be. Be. Be . . . "

I had to pee, but there were no rest areas, no gas stations. The Loneliest Highway threaded across the land of basin and range, antelope galloped across the land pocked with tumbleweeds, sagebrush, and rabbit brush. Not a spot of shade or shelter.

With a sheen of sweat on my face and neck, and as I began to think peeing my pants might not be a bad idea, a tree came into view, a giant old cottonwood. It was the only tree of any stature I'd seen in hours. I pulled over to the side of the highway beneath the tree, skin tingling as more sweat formed. The wind rustled the tree's glossy leaves, a welcome swath of green on the desert's dun palette. Looking up, I saw that every branch hung with shoes of all kinds: soccer cleats, canvas high-tops, leather work boots, shredded hiking boots. Any shoe that could be suspended from a tree branch was. I tucked my hair behind my ear. Why were the shoes there, swaying in the harsh, high-desert wind?

I hurried out of view from the road to find a place to squat and found a small arroyo behind the tree. In it lay a dead coyote. I couldn't bring myself to pee next to it. Maybe my brain was heat-addled, but it seemed disrespectful. I felt sorry for the creature decomposing alone in the arroyo beneath the only tree in a hundred miles.

———————

And so, after driving for what seemed like hours looking to find a secluded place to relieve myself, I pissed out in the open, in view of pronghorns springing past and dark-windowed automobiles whipping by. I was exposed beneath the soles of hundreds of shoes mapping their ghostly paths through the air, signs of people who had passed by that place before me.

The shoes echoed the hundreds of names I'd found in the archives of young women who had dropped out of college. Why had they left? Marriage? Pregnancy? Tragedy? Emptiness rang as the wind gusted guttural whispers in a language I couldn't understand.

Chapter 13

Post-Holing

(Fort Collins, Colorado and Davis, California)

Joy of my life, full oft for loving you
I bless my lot, that was so lucky placed...

—Edmund Spenser

I was accepted into two creative writing graduate programs: one in Fort Collins, Colorado, and one in Davis, California. I wanted to go to Colorado, where I'd be close to what I perceived as my roots and because I was attracted to the university's proximity to the rugged wilderness of the Rocky Mountains. But, I thought, if I was trying to re-invent myself—as a graduate student, as a woman newly in my thirties, as a person with something to do with her life besides wandering around mountains and deserts, maybe living in Fort Collins would thwart that goal. I decided to visit the university to help make my decision.

Driving a rented car from the Denver airport to Fort Collins along the prairie flats of the Front Range, foothills of the Rockies flanking my left side, I tried to picture myself living there, planted near the wide-open spaces and the mountains I loved equally. I checked into a Motel 6 feeling nervous about the visit, then headed to campus for meetings with the poetry professors I would work with if I chose their program.

Even at thirty, I didn't feel mature enough to converse with them the way I knew I should as a prospective graduate student. I didn't know enough about the school's creative writing program, hadn't read enough of the professors' work. I had read, written, and studied poetry as an undergraduate, but graduate school was a different game. I felt foolish. What was I doing there? I was a poetry impostor.

Despite those insecurities, I took a deep breath and stood up as tall as I could to ready myself, and walked to the graduate student poetry reading that night. As the student writers read from a small stage, I tried to imagine myself standing there in three years' time, reading aloud from the book I would produce in the program.

After the reading, there was a reception in an adjoining room, where the students greeted me. They seemed nice but understandably more caught up in their relationships with each other than in including me in their group—except for one guy.

"I'm Calvin," he said, staring overlong at my nametag. He had long, curly hair that made him look a little feral. He was deeply tanned, and he had a certain mien that every guy I'd dated had also possessed: a wilderness guy, a mountain man. "You a poet or a fiction writer?"

"Poet." I said. *Imposter*, I thought.

"I'm a poet too," he said. "So we have a lot in common."

I wondered if that could be true.

"When this party's over, you want to get a six-pack of beer and drive out to the lake and watch the stars with me?"

I rubbed my hand across my hair. I liked his offer. It allayed my feelings of loneliness and of not belonging at the event, or in graduate school. Drinking a few beers and, probably, kissing this guy in the starlight sounded good. I even allowed myself to entertain a fantasy of bringing him back to my motel room. Anything to avoid the abyss of plunging into graduate school without knowing a soul and not really having the academic background I thought I needed to pursue the degree.

But I hesitated to accept Calvin's offer, knowing it wasn't really me he wanted to drink beer with under the stars. It wasn't me he liked. I just looked like some mountain girl to him, the same way he looked like a mountain man to me. Did I want to be the poetry student who had hooked up with some guy the spring before she started the program? I didn't want to begin graduate school with that kind of baggage. Maybe for the first time in my life, my desire to be seen for who I really was overrode my desire to feel wanted. Even a month before, I might have jumped at his invitation. Something was changing for me.

"Thanks for the offer," I said, shaking my head a little. "It sounds great, but I'm tired. I'm going back to my motel."

"You sure? It would be a lot of fun." He maintained eye contact. "It's beautiful out there."

"I'm tempted," I said, digging in my coat pocket for my rental car key, "but I've got an early flight in the morning. I'll have to take a rain check. Thanks anyway."

I said goodnight to the other graduate students and walked out to my car. Feeling a little victorious, I drove alone watching the stars through my rental car windshield. He was right: they were beautiful.

––––––––––

I chose to attend graduate school in California. It was closer to Chico, where I grew up and which I considered home. I had been out of college for eight years, so it took time to adjust to my new lifestyle. I arrived in the little college town of Davis champing at the bit to start classes. But as I moved into my apartment and learned my way around the giant campus, my imposterism reared its head again, and I applied for a job with the adventure travel company run by the university's student association. It would allow me to retreat to the familiar world of leading wilderness trips that would distract me from my graduate studies. But when I was offered the job, I realized that if I was going to be a graduate student, I should fully commit to it, not divide my interests and hang onto my previous life. At the last minute, I turned down the job and instead applied to be a teaching assistant.

I was given a job reading essays for a British Literature class. Jane, the postdoctoral fellow teaching the class, was also an adoptee who hadn't found her birth parents. It was strange good fortune; until that time, I'd met few adult adoptees. I was glad I'd turned down the wilderness job to immerse myself in literature.

I sat in class listening to Jane lecture about *Ulysses* and *Women in Love*, and I enjoyed learning about British modernism. But I felt ashamed that I didn't already know these books. I read the assigned texts with a fervor, trying to keep one step ahead of the students, but I hadn't been an English major in college; I had studied sociology, anthropology, and politics. I felt woefully underprepared. It was like river kayaking—paddling through fear.

Another place I wiggled my way into was a pedagogy class for PhD students preparing to teach composition classes. I knew a degree in poetry would be difficult to parlay into gainful employment, and I knew I liked teaching because of my experience leading the poetry workshop at the international school, so I decided to take a class that would prepare me to teach college-level composition.

I was in over my head—again. My classmates were serious literature graduate students, not my creative writing cohort. The seminar met for three hours on Friday mornings. We were assigned to read stacks of articles about composition theory. I was so exhausted by being a graduate student and a teaching assistant that by the time Friday morning rolled around, I was nearly comatose, but I knew I would never catch up if I missed class, so I always went. The classroom was small and dimly lit, making it even more difficult to stay awake.

One Friday afternoon, several of my pedagogy classmates invited me to meet them at a downtown pub for beer, and I was surprised to see Andy, a literature PhD student who always sat across from me at the long seminar table. He didn't strike me as the type who would go out to a bar; he looked like the poster boy for nerdy English graduate students: pale skin, large glasses, rumpled clothes, big backpack. But he also had muscular legs that I had noticed because, unlike the other, more hip, grad students who only wore jeans, he always wore shorts.

I stood up from the patio table and walked inside to order a beer.

Blinking to adjust to the darkness in the bar, I stared up at a wall where about a hundred bottles were shelved.

Giant speakers at the back of the bar blared some old Bon Jovi song, and it echoed throughout the cavernous room.

Andy appeared next to me. "What kind of beer are you going to order?" He yelled into my ear to be heard over the music.

I did a double take. We had never spoken before. "Maybe that shark stuff over there." I raised an eyebrow and pointed to a tap that had a Great White's dorsal fin popping out of the top.

He chuckled and leaned in again to be heard. "Should we get a pitcher of 'shark stuff' for the table?"

I smiled, face flushing. I nodded and checked out his face: his bifocal lenses split his face in half horizontally, making his eyes look a little weird. But he seemed nice.

"A pitcher of 'shark-stuff,'" he called to the bartender.

Back at the patio table, I asked him what had brought him to graduate school.

"I was a lawyer for eleven years and hated it," he said, settling back in his chair.

My eyes widened. "You hated it for eleven years?" This was a guy who knew how to hold down a job, which was more than I could say; I hadn't stayed at a job for more than two years—ever. "What made you finally quit?"

He hesitated. "I got divorced, so it was a good time to make a change in my life."

Worried I'd made him uncomfortable, I busied myself pouring a glass of beer.

"I wanted to do something I felt passionate about, and I love literature," he said.

I liked him more and more. I was a little starry-eyed about the fact he'd been a lawyer—I figured it meant that he must be smart and capable to land and keep a job like that. Even better, he'd quit a presumably high-paying job to pursue his passion, which took guts.

Andy poured himself some beer and asked, "What were you doing before you started grad school?"

"Mostly working as a wilderness guide," I said.

His horizontally bisected eyes lit up. "Really? Where?"

"California, Arizona, New Mexico. Do you hike?" I assumed he didn't.

"I just finished a backpacking trip in the Pennsylvania Grand Canyon."

I snorted, spraying beer over the table. "The Pennsylvania *what?*"

I wiped up the beer with a napkin. I had never heard of that canyon. As far as I was concerned, there was only one Grand Canyon, and it was *not* in Pennsylvania.

"It's a big beautiful canyon in Pennsylvania." His brows were furrowed.

As a westerner who'd never been to Pennsylvania but had seen plenty of pictures of industrial wastelands in the Rust Belt, I could only picture sooty, coal-smoke-spewing chimneys, not beautiful canyons.

"I used to be a ranger at the Grand Canyon," I said, "and I have a feeling it is grander than any Pennsylvania Grand Canyon." I tried not to sound too arrogant, but it was difficult—I was an inveterate canyon snob.

"I've also climbed some mountains in Mexico and Ecuador." He said, leaning in.

My eyebrows shot up. Was he referring to the big, technical mountains, ones I'd dreamed of climbing but never had the guts to try?

"Popocatepetl and Cotopaxi," he said.

Those were the ones.

"When did you do that?" I took another slug of beer.

"About ten years ago. My dad was into mountain climbing for a while, and I went with him on his trips. We also trekked in Nepal and Tibet."

I was very impressed. He had done a lot of things I hadn't done, things I'd wished I could do but never had the nerve or the money to do.

"I could show you pictures sometime, if you want," he said.

——————————

A week later he picked me up at my apartment wearing a wool sport coat. I had never, ever, gone on a date with someone wearing a sport coat. It struck me as a little nerdy, but it also tickled me that he had dressed up for our date. I was accustomed to men who "dressed up" in polar fleece jackets.

We went downtown to the independent bookstore to hear local

poets read from their work, and afterward we walked to a bar to listen to some music. The lounge was dark, the band loud and not very talented. We tried to talk over the din.

"What do you think of this band?" I yelled.

"A little loud!" he yelled back, and grinned.

"Reminds me of that woman at the reading tonight who read her poem about doing meth," I replied, my voice already hoarsening with the effort of shouting. I put my hand to my throat. Andy pulled out a small pad of paper and a pen from an interior pocket of his sports coat. He wrote something on it.

"This band is awful," the note said.

I wrote back quickly: "Yeah, but it's fun—reminds me of being in college!"

"Do you think the guitarist with the pink hair is going to throw up?" he wrote. I looked up at her onstage contortions. She did look afflicted. I giggled a little.

I wrote, "Should we go for a walk before we get puked on?" and passed the notebook to him.

A look of relief washed over his face as he read.

We walked out into the night, the slight chill of late October filtering through the air. He told me more about his adventures traveling and climbing big mountains: 17,000-foot Popocatepetl, 19,000-foot Cotopaxi. He had been on mountaineering expeditions all over the world, including weeks of high-elevation trekking in India.

"What are you studying now that you're down from your high-altitude adventures?" I asked, feeling a little tingly.

"I'm a medievalist," he replied.

I laughed, picturing pimply, Dungeons-&-Dragons-playing teenage boys with long greasy hair. "Where's your velvet cape?"

His face fell. I had just insulted his life's new passion. I backpedaled. "What are you reading in your medieval seminars?"

"Dante and Chaucer. I'm also taking a Spenser seminar. We're reading *The Faerie Queene.*"

I couldn't comment. I had only read a tiny bit of Chaucer's *Canterbury Tales* and a little of Dante's *Inferno*. I had never read any Spenser.

He was quiet as he walked me back to my apartment door and left quickly. No goodnight kiss, no talk of getting together again. I knew I had offended him with the cape comment.

But the next day he emailed me a quote from *The Faerie Queene:*

```
And as she lookt about, she did behold,
How over that same dore was like wise writ,
Be bolde, be bolde, and every where Be bold,
That much she muz'd, yet could not construe it
By any ridling skill, or commune wit.
At last she spyde at that same rowmes upper end,
Another yron dore, on which was writ,
Be not too bold.
```

I smiled to myself. I had never before been flirted with in such a literary way.

We emailed every day that week; each day he relayed a quote from Chaucer or Spenser—or some other five-hundred-year-old text he was reading.

He really was a nerd, but one who had done much more interesting things in the wilderness than I had. I liked his incongruities, his sport coats for dates and baggy shorts with Teva sandals for classes; his willingness to leave a well-paid career to pursue something non-lucrative that he loved; his penchants for Old English and glacier travel. And I loved that he carried a little notebook with him in his sports coat just in case he needed to take notes on the fly. I loved that because I did it too.

After a week of emailing, he invited me to join him for pizza. I accepted, not knowing what to expect. Running my hand through my hair as I looked at myself in the mirror before I left my apartment to meet him, I wondered, *Does he like me? Does he want to get romantically involved? Do I?*

When I arrived at the little Mom-and-Pop pizza place, he greeted me from a wooden booth as he spread photographs across a rustic table. He wore no sport coat this time. "I brought those pictures I told you about," he said, sitting back in the booth.

I sat down across from him and picked up one of a little blond boy standing on a huge snowfield.

His eyes lit up. "That's me climbing Mount Rainier when I was eleven. I was the second-youngest person ever to climb it."

"You're full of surprises." I smiled at him, still trying to guess his intentions.

He laughed tentatively and picked up a picture of himself standing next to a warming hut on a mountain. "This is Popocatepetl. I got altitude sickness at fourteen thousand feet, so I stayed in that hikers' hut while my dad attempted the summit."

"He left you all by yourself with altitude sickness?" I asked. "Were you scared?"

Andy stared past my left shoulder, as if avoiding my eyes. "Not really," he said, "I think I was feeling too crappy to worry about much."

I thought about my own fear of abandonment and wondered if he'd felt that way on the mountain.

He shuffled through more pictures. "Here we are on trek in Tibet," he said, becoming animated as he arranged more photos for me to view— big mountains, round-faced, dark-skinned children staring up at the camera, colorful prayer flags.

His travels were interesting, to be sure. But I wanted to know what he wanted with me, and he was unreadable. We ate our pizza, chatted about his travels and some of mine, then parted ways, again without a kiss or any indication of his interest in me.

When I got home that night, I phoned him, my chest tight. "It was nice to see you tonight," I began.

He was silent, maybe confused about why I was calling him a half hour after seeing him.

I took a deep breath. "I'm just wondering if you're interested in dating me, or if you just want to be friends."

"Are you interested in dating me?" he countered. "Or do you just want to be friends?"

I wondered if he was a jerk or just shy. I bet on the latter and decided to shed my armor. "Yes, I'm interested in dating you," I said. "But I haven't gotten any hint from you if that's what you want."

"I'm a little gun-shy," he said. "I got really hurt in my marriage, and I've been out of the dating pool for a while."

Finally, it made sense: of course he wasn't a jerk, he was just vulnerable.

"I understand," I said. "Maybe we should make a date to kiss each other and get over that hurdle." I felt silly making this proposal, but I wanted to kiss him, and I'd been waiting for what felt like a long time.

"All right," he said, "do you want to come over to my apartment tomorrow night for a date to kiss?"

"Yes!" I said. "Do you want me to bring a couple of beers in case we need to bolster our confidence?" I added.

"Good idea, but I think I have some beers," he said. "Eight o'clock tomorrow?"

"All right. It's a kissing date." I hung up, smiling.

I arrived at his doorstep the next evening holding a bottle of beer whose label I had covered with one of my own design: it said, simply, "Courage." When he opened the door, I handed it to him wordlessly and waited to see what he would do. He smiled and invited me in, opened the beer and offered it to me.

"I'll have a sip if you have one," I said.

He smiled and took a sip, then handed the bottle to me. I slugged some down and leaned in to kiss him. And that was all it took.

A few months later, I told him about a place I wanted to take him to spend a romantic weekend—Wilbur Hot Springs, a couple hours' drive from Davis.

"There's a hotel and some good hiking," I said.

"Maybe it will stop raining long enough to actually go for a hike," he said.

That year, we had El Niño, a climate phenomenon during which the already rainy Sacramento Valley winter receives more rain than usual, waterlogging everything from December until May. In fact, that very day, after riding my bike to campus wearing full rain gear, I had to remove my shoes and pour rainwater out.

"How do you feel about being around naked people?" I said. "Most people go in the hot springs sans swimsuit."

Andy shifted his weight a little. "It's okay with me. I'm so blind without my glasses on, I probably won't even notice whether people are clothed or not."

I made a note to call Wilbur after class. I was excited about the possibility of going away with Andy to one of my favorite places. Also, I wanted to make sure he was up for experiences like this one before I let myself get serious with him. He still seemed kind of circumspect to me, despite his impressive mountain climbing resumé. He had lived most of his life in Chicago and other big cities far from the California counterculture. I needed to know if he could handle the kinds of things I liked to do.

———————

We checked into the big, old-fashioned resort hotel on Valentine's Day. The building had never been wired for electricity, so little gas lanterns hung in every room. The carpets were thick and soft, and everyone padded around in slippers. In the big industrial kitchen, a holdover from the days when the inn had a restaurant, guests cooked meals wearing bathrobes. Outside the lobby window the multiple pools of hot water steamed up the winter air.

We took a quiet room with rough-hewn wooden walls and a skylight, through which I could see the deeply lobed leaves of valley oaks. They cast undulating shadows across the purple bedspread. It felt very romantic, but we decided to go out for a hike right away because, by some miracle, the sun was out for the first time in weeks.

———————

We walked along a trail dense with oak trees, and the sun shone on us and all the leaves, making the wet world sparkle like a kept promise. I breathed in the air hungrily, as if I hadn't been outside in years, thrilled to finally be out in the sunshine and chatting with the man I was falling for, and to have a weekend with no studying or grading papers.

The trail exited the woods and the landscape opened up into pastureland dotted with grazing cattle. We hiked along until the trail turned back toward the inn.

I didn't want to go back yet. "Let's hike cross country," I said. "It's wide open here—we'll be able to see where we're going. We should be able to find our way back pretty easily."

Andy agreed, and I took his hand. We hiked side by side for a while, tromping over the rangeland. The grasses were deliciously electric green, and my eyes dazzled after many months of gray rain and leafless trees in Davis. I was so happy that I practically skipped along.

We crested a small hill, and as we reached the lowest area of the field on the other side, our feet sank into the sod with each step. We were in a bog. I slowed down and let go of Andy's hand, trying to keep my balance and avoid getting my boots stuck in the mud.

It started to rain. After a few minutes, I looked over my shoulder at Andy, a few yards behind me, and asked, "How are you doing?"

He didn't answer right away. He pushed his glasses up his nose. They slipped right back down. "Not too well," he said. "I can't see. My glasses keep falling down my face and I don't have my eyeglass leash."

The missing eyeglass leash had dancing Rastafarian men inked on it in red, green, and yellow. It seemed like a silly choice for an Irish-skinned, folk-music-loving white man to wear, and I had teased him about it.

"You don't really want to wear these, do you?" I had asked, dangling them just out of his reach at his apartment the previous day.

"I do. They keep my glasses on so I can see," he said.

"I think you can get along without them," I said, and I kissed him as I stuffed the leash into my pocket.

"If my face gets wet, my glasses don't stay on very well."

"You'll be fine," I said, kissing him again to distract him. "Let's go!"

As I had with every other boyfriend, I was testing him, pushing him to see how he would react. So far, he seemed unflappable.

But now, in the pouring rain and miles from the hotel, his hair hung in his reddening face, and his breathing was shallow. I tried to imagine what it was like for him to slog through the mud with limited vision, feet sinking deeply with each step, making post-hole-sized indentions. Definitely not fun. I felt terrible; I was having a great time and he was not, and it was my fault.

"I'm sorry I stole your leash," I said. "We can still do this. We'll take it slower. You could try stepping in the holes I've already made."

He made a grumbly noise. "I think we should start looking for a way back."

I agreed and headed for what looked like a creek in the distance. It was still raining hard.

Muddy and soaked to the skin in spite of all our rain gear, we trudged the rest of the way through the boggy field to a creek, then followed it back toward the hot springs, the creek bed's wet metamorphic rocks clinking as our boots hit them.

Andy looked around and stopped walking. "I think the hotel is on the other side."

We both stared at the rain-swollen creek. Every time I'd been there before, it had been a mild-mannered trickle, but El Niño's storms had bloated it into a raging river.

"I guess we could hike back out toward the road where there's a bridge," I said. "Or we could just keep going in this direction and hope we can get across."

"Let's head back toward the road," he said, his hood on, glasses teetering at the very tip of his nose, and face speckled with raindrops. He looked a little like the Muppet named Beaker.

Guilt spread throughout my guts like food poisoning.

"The bridge is the better bet," I said, turning around and starting to trudge back down the creek bed. I hesitated, then reached for Andy's hand again. He let me take it, surprising me a little. I squeezed his hand, which was wet but warm. We hiked along in the rain holding hands for another hour until we found the bridge, crossed it, and turned to hike back on the other side of the creek.

When we finally reached the hotel, dusk was falling, the valley hushed and glowing lavender. The rain had reduced itself to a sprinkle. Sulfur fumes from the hot springs wafted around us, and Andy wrinkled his nose.

We walked directly to the springs, peeled off our layers of saturated clothing, and slipped into one of the steamy pools, where several other people sat quietly. Naked.

"That's better," I said, my rain-puckered skin flushing with heat.

"Are all the hikes you take like that?" Andy said. "Or were you just trying to haze me?" Although signs reminding visitors to be silent hung throughout the pool area, I couldn't help laughing out loud. Andy knew hazing when he saw it.

I turned and smiled at him, giggling nervously, my shoulders shaking and splashing the water around us. The water rippled over to a woman with her eyes closed and sloshed onto her chin. She abruptly opened her eyes, looked around to determine what was going on. I smiled at her apologetically, then turned back to Andy.

"I won't do it anymore," I whispered.

"Good," he said, and he scooted a little closer to me in the pool.

―――――――――

At the start of our second year of graduate school, we moved into a little house on the east side of town. Even though it was difficult to find time for outdoor adventures while classes were in session, we managed to backpack in Yosemite, Hawaii, and Utah during the summers. He continued to woo me with quotations from medieval authors.

I knew this was a man who would not leave me. He proposed and I accepted.

Chapter 14

Facts and Artifacts

(On the Colorado River through the Grand Canyon)

It's a sensation of hunger
That makes us spring off the bottom and swim out deep
And safe.

—Sandra McPherson

I wanted to paddle a raft 279 miles through the Grand Canyon for our honeymoon. I imagined whitewater rearing up before me, taunting me, daring me to have a good marriage, and testing myself against it, committing to its entirety.

Rafting seemed like an apt metaphor for our marriage: awe-inspiring and fun if we didn't let fear get in the way, and essential to dig in our paddles and pull our way through it together when the water got rough.

I wanted to leave everything behind, dig in with Andy, and emerge changed, whole.

My Ankylosing Spondylitis had flared up terribly during the months before our wedding. Maybe it was the stress of planning, or maybe it was just the disease's quixotic behavior. For months, I had been in so much pain I'd barely been able to go to work, much less exercise. I was scared of how bad it might get and desperate for a sense of control over the disease.

So, I looked to the river trip as a way to defeat the pain. Maybe I could paddle it away, push it behind.

Andy and I sat in the living room of our house, clicking through commercial rafting websites.

"I want us to face that whitewater together," I said, pointing at a picture on the screen of a group of people with paddles sunk into churning water. "Oar trips are too passive—when I did it before, I just sat there and watched the canyon go by."

Andy pulled up a list. "Look at the price tag on that. I don't think we can afford it."

I looked, scrunched my face. "We definitely can't afford it," I said. "We're graduate students. But let's find a way to make it work. It's important. It's my one and only honeymoon." I glanced over at him. Andy was my family now, and I wanted to share with him the place that meant so much to me. I wanted him to see how the Grand Canyon was a home, albeit a complicated one. I wanted it to be his too.

"I might be able to tap some savings," he said. "Call in a few favors."

I grabbed his hand. "Let's do it!" I squeezed hard. "I can take on extra work somewhere."

We were married in an oak forest near Chico. Now assimilated to California style, Andy didn't wear a sport coat—or any coat—and only at the last minute deigned to put on a tie. My friend Marci of the Alaska adventures officiated, and dear friends read poetry to us in the July dusk. Small children of our friends played in the grass while we danced, and I was very happy.

Before we left on our road trip to the Grand Canyon, I mailed the paperwork to the state of Colorado asking them to appoint an independent searcher on my behalf. I had waited a decade to do it, not wanting to pay the five-hundred-dollar fee for access to information that I felt was mine—my sealed records, my original, unamended birth certificate. But

I had finally given in after my amateur search garnered nothing, and I sat on that nothing for years.

Maureen, the woman from the archives in Greeley, had emailed me a few times. Incredibly, she had continued helping me search, visiting public libraries in Colorado and looking in old yearbooks. She even researched small towns with girls' swim teams but found none. There were no girls' sports in those days. That "fact" about my birth mother from the non-identifying information appeared to have been fabricated by the adoption agency.

I didn't know what else to ask Maureen to look for. As for the two hundred names I'd highlighted in yellow on the Greeley college enrollment rosters, I didn't have the guts or the stamina to track them all down. By the time I submitted the application to participate in the confidential intermediary program, I had swallowed my anger and hoped that my birth mother would want contact with me if the searcher found her.

Andy and I drove to northeastern Arizona, where we met our guides and fellow passengers at a roadside inn near the Glen Canyon Dam. We sat on a fireplace hearth holding hands and looking around at twenty people squeezed into the room. I was going to be in the Grand Canyon for two weeks, uninterrupted by work, computers, bills, with no obligation other than to paddle with Andy at my side. And I was confident we would emerge safely, and together, at the end of the trip, unlike Bessie and Glen Hyde on their honeymoon.

It was obvious to me which people were our river guides. They were tanned and rugged, wore sun-faded clothes. Sam, the trip leader, sported long golden hair and a tattered tennis visor. Barb looked to be in her forties, with graying hair and an impish, weathered smile. Craig's tan was so dark that his teeth shone like a Cheshire cat's.

I had looked like them when I was a guide. But I was no longer part of their crowd. My fellow passengers and I wore clean, wide-brimmed shade hats and nylon shorts so new, they practically squeaked when we walked.

My heart ached. I couldn't help wishing I could dive back into a lifestyle of adventure and freedom. I'd made a choice to move on, but I felt the pull of wilderness. That Expansive Canyon Feeling buoyed my ribcage.

Several days into the trip, some of us woke extra early to hike up Tapeats Creek to a voluminous spring pumping straight out of a canyon wall, ninety feet up. Sparse rock overhangs shaded us a little as we hiked across gritty sandstone to the site of some ancient dwellings.

I picked up a potsherd from the ground and showed it to Andy. "It's like they were just here."

Andy took the broken piece of pottery and smoothed it between his thumb and forefinger. He gently replaced it on the ground.

Most of our group returned to the boats after the waterfall, but Sam guided a few of us willing to brave the heat across Surprise Valley, a basin that didn't drain anything anymore. Andy and I plodded across the desert side by side, barely speaking as the day grew hotter. I thought my body might crack open and fall to the ground in a pile of smoking dust. The only shade along the five-mile stretch was cast by a lone sandstone boulder, so we rested in its meager shadow, willing our brains to cool, pouring precious drinking water from our bottles down our necks.

Finally cooled off enough to think, I realized that, during the trip, my joint pain had eased for the first time in months. Maybe it was the arid climate or the physical exertion of paddling all day every day, maybe the relative lack of stress of being on vacation. Or the pure joy of living in the canyon for two weeks.

We hiked back to the boats along Deer Creek drainage. Sam pointed out a gap in the Redwall Limestone that had filled with crushed rock.

"I think the Colorado River once flowed through there," he said, panting in the heat. "And carved lower Deer Creek into a narrow slot canyon." He stopped walking to pull a ragged T-shirt out of a trailside cactus's spines and jammed the sun-bleached fabric into a side pocket of his backpack. I stared up at the fill, wondering what stories lay buried beneath it.

Farther downstream, we spied reverse-handprint pictographs: outlined in white, ghostly and small. They looked like cherished baby handprints cast in plaster and hung on a living room wall. I took Andy's hand between both of mine and held on for a minute.

In that desert, every ancient human tool came from the soil: clay, paint, yucca fibers, mortared rock granaries and dwellings. I sought tools for finding my birth parents. My skin prickled every time I thought about the application I'd sent to the confidential intermediary program, imagining what might be happening. Maybe they would find my birth mother while I was away. Maybe she lived somewhere near the Grand Canyon.

Back in our boats, we paddled through Doris and Fishtail Rapids and tied up the rafts for the night at Kanab Creek Canyon, where in 1872 some of the men on John Wesley Powell's second Grand Canyon river expedition departed, traveling sixty miles in three days from the Colorado River to the town of Kanab, Utah.

Thomas Moran, renowned artist, visited and sketched landscapes of the beach and canyons of Kanab Creek. I sat alone in that storied place on an unusual, humid evening, listening to mice rustle through the willows, feeling the tickle of ants crawling over my feet as I watched the river curl its way downstream.

I knew what was there; I had rafted it before, but I had a feeling it would be different this time, and different again the next time I traveled it.

For the rest of the trip I scanned side canyons, ledges, and alcoves, cottonwood branches and agave leaves, redbuds' pink pea blossoms, seeking equanimity. Without knowing how it would look or feel, I could only hope I would know it when I found it.

I knew it wouldn't be something I'd pick from the riverbank, a slick shard of shale or an ancient arrowhead, but a calm I could take home with me, like sitting on sand in shade after a long hot day of hiking. I took solace that despite the Glen Canyon Dam upstream, the river still flowed. Sometimes it even flowed clear.

———————

After two weeks on the river, Andy and I toured the Glen Canyon Dam—a crime scene pilgrimage. I wanted to see the behemoth that had changed the river so much. We rode a glass elevator deep into the dam's whirring belly of generators and turbines. Before, I had thought the dam was a static tower of cement but now I saw that it was a huge machine, almost a living thing. It made me shiver.

At its massive concrete base, we exited the elevator. Looking up at the span of concrete abutting the sandstone cliffs, I tugged hard on Andy's sleeve and pointed up at the wall.

"The cliffs are dripping with water from behind the dam." My heart beat quickly.

Andy looked up, adjusted his glasses. "The river water must've saturated the sandstone."

"That seems unsafe." I noticed long metal rods had been hammered into the rock, stabilizing the sandstone. But water seeped through, sluicing down the canyon walls to create a small cascade. "Looks like it could give way at any moment," I said, feeling breathless.

"Very weird," said Andy. "I wonder how long it's been like that."

He walked over to a tour guide, a young Native woman wearing a uniform with the badge of the Natural History Association on it. I stood near the waterfall, eyebrows furrowed. *How could the Glen Canyon Dam possibly be considered a part of natural history?* I wondered. *It's anything but natural.*

"She says it's been like that for decades." The spray from the waterfall misted Andy's face as he approached me. "And it's not a problem."

I looked up again, pursing my lips. After fifteen days living under the river's spell, I wanted erosion to prevail over the dam.

———————

We took the elevator back to the top of the dam and got in our car for the long drive home. I sighed, stared out the windshield thinking about sandstone's process: deposition, deposition, deposition, rain, heat, wind, compression. Inland seas form; horseshoe crabs skim sea beds, leave cryptic tracks; seas recede. Dunes form hundreds of feet deep. Wind. More deposition, more water, more heat. Stillness. Then a dam is built. Then the waiting.

I sighed again. *It can't hold much longer.*

Chapter 15

Intermediary

(Davis, California)

And there is the land, looming, mountainous, massive...
On the horizon: there in our minds.

—Alicia Ostriker

A ndy unpacked the car as I gathered the pile of mail that had arrived while we were gone. My whole body tingled. The letter on top was from the Colorado Confidential Intermediary Program. I tore it open and read that they had assigned a searcher to my case, but she was at work on other cases, and I would have to wait. Probably months. My jaw went slack.

The searcher, Shirley, phoned me in December to tell me it was my turn, that she'd start working on my case. For days after the call, I couldn't focus on any task, anything.

On day seven, she called again to say she'd found my birth mother. *Seven days.* For ten years, I had searched and pined and cried and racked my brain for how to find her, and Shirley had found her in a week. I cursed myself for waiting so long to try the intermediary program, for wasting so much time.

"How did you do it?" I asked her, rushing to get the words out. "I tried everything I could think of."

"She used a false name on your original birth certificate," Shirley said. "I was only able to find her because your maternal grandfather signed some of the adoption paperwork, and I noticed that his last name was different than the one your birth mother used, so I pursued his name and found his daughter, your birth mother."

I grew quiet, wondering why she had used a fake name—had it been her idea or someone else's? Had she been forced to do it?

Shirley wasn't allowed to disclose my birth mother's name or anything else that would identify her, but she was able to confirm some facts I had ferreted out during my searching: my birth mother had indeed attended college in Greeley for one semester before withdrawing because she was visibly pregnant. And, as I suspected, I had been born at the Florence Crittenden Home for Unwed Mothers in Denver.

"I don't want to contact your birth mother right away," Shirley said. "I'm sorry. I know you've been waiting a long time."

My heart sank. Why did we have to wait? Had she uncovered some terrible secret?

"The holidays are almost here, and she may have family or guests staying with her. Generally, it's not a good idea for me to contact people around Christmas, so I'd like to wait until early January to call her."

It felt like a cruel prank. Now I knew my birth mother had been found, but I didn't know if she *wanted* to be found, and I would have to wait weeks to get an answer. I knew Shirley was just trying to give me the best chance at a positive outcome, so I thanked her and tried to get off the phone before she could hear my voice shaking.

———————

I became irritable, withdrawn, sleepless. One night, Andy and I went to see a movie in which a terrified man who has just survived a jetliner's crash into the ocean floats in a small yellow life raft in the dark sea, his boat a tiny disk spinning among huge swells. Until that moment, I had been unable to express how it felt to wait to find out if my birth mother was willing to know me, or if she would reject me again.

I shook Andy's shoulder and pointed at the screen. "THAT," I whispered loudly, trying not to yell, "is EXACTLY how I feel!"

He gave me a quizzical look, then nodded and rubbed my back, obviously unsure of what to say.

After the movie, we walked home through a cold fog, coats buttoned up to our chins.

"Did you see how that raft was spinning out of control?" I said. "How huge the waves were, like there was nothing but rough water and darkness in the world?" I gestured in wide arcs, stopped walking and waited for him to respond.

"I did," he said slowly, stopping and curling his arm around me as he had in the theatre.

"Well, can you understand that my life feels like that right now? Anything could happen! Maybe something terrible!"

"I'm trying to understand." He gently nudged me onward along the sidewalk.

"Then why won't you talk to me about it?" My voice quavered. "I feel horrible. I feel like I'm going to throw up all the time. I need your help."

"I'm right here for you," he said, sounding a little tense.

I wanted to punch him. He was *not* right there for me. He was a million miles away—on solid ground.

We walked the rest of the way home in silence.

After that, I stopped asking him for support. I remained in a funk for the rest of December. At Christmas and New Year's parties I floated in my dark and roiling sea, feeling misunderstood. It was hard to talk to friends about what was going on. Those who knew I had been searching for a long time understood that finding my biological parents was important to me, but when I told them Shirley had found my birth mother, their excited responses fell and clattered at my feet. I couldn't explain how awful I felt, how scared I was, how unmoored. All I could do in response to their support was recount the scene from the movie of the shipwrecked man spinning in his boat. Most looked at me the same way Andy had: sympathetic but uncomprehending.

On January eighth, Shirley called and told me it was time. She asked if I had a message I wanted to relay to my birth mother. Hoping that a personal touch would increase the chances she'd respond positively to Shirley's news, I wrote an email, cramming in everything I could think of about myself while I tried to ignore the butterflies in my stomach:

Dear Shirley,

I'd like my birth mother to know that I'm okay. I'd also like her to know what I look like: I'm 5'4" tall and have straight, sandy blond hair and greenish-brown eyes. I'd also like her to know what I like to do: I like to hike, swim, and write. I have a master's degree in creative writing, and I teach at a university in California. And I used to be a wilderness guide.

My husband, whom I met in graduate school, is working on a PhD in English literature. We married last July, and we live with our dog. We're hoping to have kids in the next few years.

I'd like her to know that I'm not angry with her for placing me for adoption, and that I have much empathy for how difficult it must have been to go through a pregnancy as an unmarried woman in the '60s, and that I'm sad she had to do something as difficult as giving up a child for adoption when she was so young.

Most of all, I want her to know that if we were to have contact, I wouldn't call upon her as a parent; I just want to know what she looks like, what she likes to do, how her life has turned out.

```
I want her to know that I understand the idea
of contact with me may seem overwhelming, but I
hope she'll choose to do it anyway. And please
let her know that I'm willing to do it in incre-
mental stages if that's less daunting to her.
And although I'd be very sad if she didn't want
contact, I'd understand if she felt unable. I'd
like to make a connection with her that I cannot
fully put into words. I can only hope that she
understands I'm missing something important,
and that something important is to know her.
```

I hit "Send."

I hurried out the front door and walked around the foggy town, silently asking whomever might be listening to please, please, let my birth
mother accept me. I repeated my mute plea for hours, afraid that if I
stopped, I'd lose any chance of ever knowing where I had come from.

I once read in an article about taxonomy that studies suggest there might
be a specific part of the brain devoted to it, implying that our tendency
to name and classify the world around us is evolutionary and integral to
our humanness. The studies also showed that people who have damage
to the taxonomic area of the brain are "completely at sea. Without the
power to order and name life, a person simply does not know how to live
in the world, how to understand it.... They are utterly lost, anchorless
in a strange and confusing world. Because to order and name life is to
have a sense of the world around, and as a result, what one's place is in it."
This made perfect sense to me. As a creative writing teacher, I often told
my classes that poetry is the act of renaming the world. As an adopted
person, I knew the power of names and the lack thereof. Naming and renaming the world are acts of creation; when something is named, it is
brought into being.

I felt I could only heal from the loss of my original family by naming
it: Kingdom, Phylum, Class, Order, *Family*, Genus, Species. Naming and

knowing it might be the only thing that could make me feel like a real human person with a past, not just a Floating Space Baby. Perhaps, then, it was no coincidence that I became a poet; having grown up not knowing my own name, I was compelled to rename the world around me.

I didn't have to wait much longer for the naming to begin. Shirley called back later in the day. "I spoke with your birth mother, and she said she would be happy to have contact with you."

A tingling feeling rushed through my body. I yelped a little, then thanked her, and began firing questions. "Where does she live? Is she married? Does she have other children?"

In a quiet voice, Shirley told me what she'd learned, obviously experienced with adoption reunion participants' need for information. I could hear the pleasure in her voice when she relayed the first facts I ever got about my birth mother: "She's married, has two grown children, and lives in Indiana. And she works at a library. She sounds like a very nice lady."

This information thrilled me, and it opened up more questions: Had she told anyone about me? Had she searched for me? Were her parents alive? What did she look like? I was an infant learning about her mother— over the phone, at age thirty-three.

Shirley wasn't allowed to give me names or phone numbers yet. She had to file my birth mother's written consent with the state courts of Colorado, and then that consent would have to be verified by a judge.

———————————

I spent a month daydreaming about our first contact as red tape unraveled its way from Colorado to somewhere in Indiana and back to Colorado again: *Should I call or write her?* I wondered. A letter seemed the most appropriate for that momentous occasion, but after waiting so long, I wanted immediacy. I wanted to talk to her on the phone, to hear her voice and breath, to hear her laugh or cry, to detect if we had anything in common.

Two weeks into the wait, Shirley emailed me a scanned copy of a handwritten note from my birth mother, thanking Shirley for connecting us. My birth mother's signature at the end of the note was redacted, so she was still anonymous to me, but I fixated on the neat loops of her handwriting, reading and rereading her words of thanks as if trying to decipher any code that might be hidden in them, the way I had spent time scrutinizing pictographs in the Grand Canyon.

I fell in love with my birth mother by tracing her written words with my eyes, her words not even meant for me.

———————

Weeks later, Shirley was allowed to tell me my birth mother's name: Elaine.

I rolled it over in my mouth, wondering who she was and if she had named me when I was born. I wrote "Elaine" in my notebook. What to do next? I desperately wanted to talk to her, but I didn't know how to start.

"I don't want to call Elaine without warning," I told Shirley. "I want her to be ready, to have time to sit down and talk for a while. What should I do?"

"Would you like me to ask her when would be a good time for you to call?"

I felt like a junior high school kid asking a friend to ask the boy I liked if he liked me too. Shirley said she'd give Elaine a ring and get back to me.

My phone rang again a few minutes later.

"Elaine said you can call right now, if you want," Shirley said. "She said she's just watching a ball game."

I got off the phone and sat in silence for a few moments, heart pounding, a little stunned by my birth mother's nonchalance about the phone call. I heard Andy in the next room tapping away at his computer, trying to finish a chapter of his dissertation.

"She said I could call right now!" I yelled. "What should I do?"

Andy walked into the room, a big smile on his face. "Call her."

Part Three

Navel of the World

Chapter 16

First Words

(Davis, California)

each rock a word
a creek-washed stone

—Gary Snyder

I fiddled with a pencil jar on my desk, which was strewn with untidy stacks of poems and student essays I hadn't finished grading.

"Elaine?" I asked, staring at a brand-new pad of paper, upon which I planned to take notes during our conversation so I wouldn't miss anything she said.

"Is this Andrea?" Her voice was full and melodic, a little familiar—perhaps a bit like mine. I realized I expected her to sound meek, contrite. I thought maybe we'd start where we had left off decades ago, with her regret. Or at least what I imagined was her regret.

"It is!" I said, trying to sound both upbeat and casual, but wanting to say *Where have you been all these years? Why didn't you find me?*

"How are you, dear?" *Am I dear to her, really?* My head felt like it was going to explode from exercising restraint. *How did you do it? How could you give me away?*

"We're just sitting here watching college basketball. The Hoosiers are playing. It's another snowy night in Indiana," said Elaine, her voice revealing a faint southern accent. *Right, Indiana's almost in the South.*

"It's cold here too," I said, "but it doesn't snow in this part of California. It just gets rainy and foggy." She didn't say, "I'm so glad you found me! I've missed you so much," or even "I can't believe I'm actually speaking with you after all these years." She wasn't saying the things I wanted so badly to hear. But then, neither was I.

"I'll you a little about my family," Elaine said. "My daughter, Tanya, graduated last May from Indiana University, and my son, Matt, is in college in Muncie."

"I have a sister and a brother," I wrote. I tried to picture them—did they look like me? I'd never had a sister, had always wanted one. I quickly did the math—I was eleven years older than my new half sister.

"Tanya and I are very close," Elaine said. "We talk on the phone almost every day." Why did she tell me that? To make me jealous? To show me what a good mother she was? Because she was nervous? I tried to remember how often I had talked to my mom on the phone when I was Tanya's age. I didn't think it was every day. What did that mean about my relationship with my mom?

I tried to keep the conversation going while scribbling down what Elaine said. It was difficult to do both—and to process it. My brain felt both full and blank. I realized the only way I was going to get through this conversation feeling safe was to dam up my feelings, like Elaine seemed to be doing.

"Tanya likes exercising," Elaine continued. "Both my kids were really into swim team when they were growing up." Hearing about her athletic kids made me feel a little envious; I had never competed in sports, probably because I didn't have the self-confidence to do it.

"I swim too," I said. "Not competitively, though. Just for exercise." I sat up in my desk chair. "What do your kids look like?"

"Oh, they're tall. Matt's six-foot-one and Tanya's five-foot-seven. They both look like their dad, my husband Luke. They have his blue eyes and dark hair."

I ached with disappointment. They didn't look like me at all. I longed to meet someone who looked like me, and I had been hoping that Elaine or one of her children would.

"Do they know about me?" I asked, surprised at my own daring. It was the first thing I'd managed to say that hinted at the secrecy and shame of our situation.

Elaine paused. "I told Tanya a few years ago. But Matt doesn't know." Another pause. Her voice brightened, "Now that you and I are in contact, I'm going to call him and tell him."

Why hasn't she already told him? What kind of Pandora's box am I opening? What disruption will that phone call cause?

"How do you think he'll take it?" I asked, squirming in my seat.

The triple conversation—what I said, what she told me, and what I was thinking—made my head feel like it was haunted by howling ghosts.

"Oh, I imagine he'll be surprised. He thinks I'm such a straight arrow." She cleared her throat. "How many siblings do you have?"

There was a story there. I wondered what it was, but I didn't have the guts to ask her why she hadn't told Matt or why he thought she was a "straight arrow."

"I have two brothers, both younger," I answered, struggling to process what she'd just said, and what she hadn't. The ghosts in my head kept up their lament.

"That's nice," she replied. "I was an only child. I always wanted brothers and sisters. I barely had any cousins."

I already knew she was an only child. Now it seemed she had been a lonely one. It was difficult to keep from completely drifting out of the conversation and into my own musings.

She, too, seemed to be struggling to keep the conversation going. "What was your maiden name?" she asked.

"I kept my maiden name when I got married," I said, noting that she assumed I had changed it. *Will she judge me for not being traditional?* I wondered.

"Oh! I see," she said.

Is she trying to suppress her surprise at my choice?

"Your last name, is it Scottish?"

"My dad's family is Scottish. My mom's family is Finnish—Lutheran Finns." I felt the squeeze of religious expectation clamp down on my stomach. I had known this topic would come up at some point; after all, she had placed me with a Lutheran adoption agency, so I figured she was religious.

"Were you raised Lutheran?" she asked.

My stomach clamped even more. "Yes, but I don't attend church anymore," I said. "You're Lutheran, right?"

"Yes," she said, "we're very active in the church. I'm on some committees and such."

I noted this difference between us, writing "still Lutheran" in my notebook.

Perhaps sensing my uneasiness with the topic of religion, she changed the subject again. "I imagine you want to know about your medical history."

"Yes, I really do," I said, trying not to sound overeager.

"Well, we're all very healthy," she said. "My mother lived until she was ninety. She was very strong."

I was surprised to hear it. I had expected she might have something like the disease I inherited. I tried to breathe a little more deeply and picture my strong, healthy, ninety-year-old birth grandmother.

"She was a wonderful woman. She just died about a year ago. I know she would have wanted to meet you." Once again, Elaine paused. "She came down to the maternity home to see you the morning you were born."

My breath caught. Elaine had recently lost her mother, and I had missed meeting her by a year. I wondered if the death of her mother had opened Elaine to finding me. I stared at my hands, hoping my grandmother had held me at the maternity home.

Realizing I had been silent too long, I said, "I would've liked to meet her too." I tried to envision her touching my baby skin, holding my horizontal form to her chest knowing she'd never see me again.

"She did have osteoporosis," Elaine said, pulling me back into the present. "It runs in our family."

I wrote "Osteoporosis: source of my back pain?"

"Her back hurt a lot," Elaine continued. "She always carried this little pillow around to put behind her when she sat down. Now that I think about it, so did my grandmother."

I wrote that down too, thinking the pain must've been pretty bad if they carried pillows everywhere they went.

"What about your father? Is he still alive?" I asked.

"He died eleven years ago from an intestinal blockage. It was non-cancerous."

I scribbled that down, brows furrowed. Elaine's idea of "very healthy" was quite different from mine.

"My father's last name was Feiring," she said. "It's a Norwegian name, an unusual one. All my grandparents were Norwegian. My paternal grandmother came over from Norway in 1908," Elaine said. "I'd love to go to Norway sometime."

"Me too." I said, pulse quickening. "Maybe we could go together."

My brain spun wildly: *I'm half Norwegian—what does it mean to finally verify that part of my identity? What about the other half? Where was my birth father from? Who was he? Will she tell me?* I was becoming overwhelmed, finding it difficult to think clearly. I didn't have the nerve to ask her about my birth father.

"That would be nice," she said slowly. I winced, wondering if I had overstepped, if she found me laughable. My face burned.

The conversation limped along, each of us learning bits about the other's life, neither one broaching the subject of adoption, of loss, of one person giving up on another. But the voices in my head howled all the questions I'd had for thirty-three years.

Stomach churning, I asked, "Did you name me when I was born?"

"Yes, I did," she replied quietly. "Melinda Dawn Ericsson."

My heart jumped. I had a baby name.

"I loved the name Melinda," Elaine said softly. "And Ericsson was my great-grandmother's last name." She paused. "My father didn't want anyone to trace the adoption to us, so I used Ericsson as your last name."

"Melinda," I wrote, as if addressing a letter to myself. I had never known anyone with that name. It felt strange to know that Elaine had thought of me as Melinda all those years, that I indeed had a name—and maybe a place—in her mind. But her father had wanted to erase all evidence of my link to her and his family. I shifted in my chair.

"I'm glad you found me," said Elaine.

Words I had been dying to hear. Tears flooded my eyes.

"I tried to find you about ten years ago," she said. "I called the adoption agency and asked how I could contact you, but they told me it wasn't allowed, so I didn't try after that."

My heart raced. Had she really tried? And if she had, what did the social workers at the agency really say to her? Weren't the letters from my parents and me in my file by that time?

"Ten years ago," I managed to say despite the maelstrom in my head. "That's about when I started trying to find you. What a coincidence." I tried to calm myself, to not show how hurt I was. "That's about when I got my non-identifying information from the adoption agency."

Elaine remained silent.

I looked around my room, hoping for distraction from the pain of that lost decade but finding only blank cream-colored walls. What might have happened if she'd found me when I was twenty-three? So much of the pain I'd experienced could have been avoided. But I was a different person at that age. Maybe I wouldn't have been ready for this.

I laid myself bare. "It said you liked to write poetry and that you were on a swim team. I've always wondered if that's why I like to write and swim, if I got those things from you."

"A swim team?" she asked. "I was never on one. I don't think they even had teams for girls when I was in high school. At least not at my high school."

I choked, tried to catch my breath quietly. The agency had lied. Or had Elaine's father? Either way, I had believed it. I had concocted countless daydreams about my birth mother, the swimmer. And Maureen and I had spent hours trying to track down girls' swim teams in 1960s Colorado, but it was all a lie. My face flushed with anger. Or was it sorrow? My head hurt.

"What about poetry?" I asked, afraid to hear the answer.

"Oh, I don't know," she said. "I suppose I might have done a little writing in high school, but it wasn't a big thing for me."

Another bit of "inherited" identity I'd clung to for many years was not inherited at all. I wondered how much of the information I'd obtained from the adoption agency was fraudulent. I felt foolish. I had cultivated my interests, my identity, based on made-up information. I was a sucker. I felt even less sure of my identity than before I talked to Elaine.

I changed the subject. Shirley had told me Elaine worked at a library, so I figured it was safe to assume that we shared a love of books and read-ing. "I think Shirley said you're a librarian?" I said.

"Oh no, I'm a bookkeeper at the county library. I do love to check out books on tape, though."

"Me too," I said weakly, wondering why it was so hard to get accurate secondhand information. But now it was I who was lying. I didn't like books on tape; I liked real books. I loved reading—touching actual books and reading their delicious words from tangible pages. "Did you go to col-lege to be a teacher?" I asked, still relying on the information I'd obtained a decade ago, hoping to forge a bond.

"My mother was a teacher, and I wanted to be a teacher too. I finished college and got my teaching credential. After you were born. But I never worked as a full-time teacher. I just did some substituting. Then I got mar-ried and had kids, so . . ." her voice trailed off.

I continued scribbling notes about everything she said, not wanting to miss anything. But I wondered who this woman was to me, what she could become, where we would go from here.

"Now that I finally have your address," I said. "I'd like to send you some pictures. Of myself, my husband, my family. Would that be okay?"

"Oh, yes!" she exclaimed. "Please do. I'd really like to see what you look like."

I was dying to know what she looked like. I wanted us to look alike. My stomach ached with need. "Will you send me pictures of yourself and your family?"

"Of course, honey," she said.

Honey. It was so motherly. Did she feel that for me, or was she just curious and nothing more? I didn't know where to put my emotions, so they all rushed to my belly, making it hurt.

We got off the phone, promising to send pictures and call again soon. I sat, motionless, for a few moments.

I dug through my closet for photos to tell the story of my life, ones that would make her want to become a part of it. I looked for pictures that showed me as adventurous, strong and brave, not the way I really felt. I found a photo of my twenty-five-year-old self, hair in long braids, wearing my giant backpack. I stood beside a creek in the High Sierra, grinning and pointing at an orange tiger lily. I loved those flowers, their unexpected blaze of color in the verdure of forest, their delicate curled petals. When that picture was taken, a friend and I had been checking out a route for a ten-day women's wilderness leadership course we were planning. That summer I slept more nights outside than inside, which was how I liked it.

But seeing that image of my radiant joy and youthful strength in the backcountry didn't override my uneasiness about not finding connection with Elaine. I pulled another photograph from the album—a pre-dawn moment as I sat on a glacier, strapping crampons to my boots, preparing to attempt the summit of Mount Shasta in northern California. Shasta was a beacon in my childhood landscape. At just over 14,000 feet, it was visible from most places I traveled, its massive presence anchoring me in the relative wilds of far-northern California. In the photo, I smiled, squinty-eyed with fatigue after a restless night in the cold and ferocious wind below the summit. To the untrained eye, I looked like I knew what I was doing, but I was an amateur: too inexperienced to know to rise earlier to have enough time to melt enough snow for the day's drinking water, unconfident in my ability to self-arrest with my ice axe if I slid down a snow bank.

Did I want to spin a tale of my adventurous outdoor life for Elaine, or did I want to show her how different we were? I hadn't selected photos of myself watching sporting events, or serving food at church potlucks, or listening to audiobooks. I didn't have those kinds of photos. I wanted my pictures to make her wish she had known me all those years. To make her love me.

But what did she want? She had given me only limited clues. Did she wonder if I loved her? If I missed her? I had spent years longing for communion with her, but in that first phone conversation, I only found tiny bits of it. There was no epiphany that settled my queries about identity. I had not been visited by a sudden feeling of rootedness, the kind I always felt when I glimpsed Mount Shasta in the rearview mirror of my car. I only had more questions: *Where do we go from here? How do we navigate this unmapped landscape? Now that I am real to her, who am I?*

Chapter 17

The Navel of the World

(Davis, California)

we listened to photographs. They heard our voice speak.

—Barbara Guest

On a rainy afternoon in February, weeks after my first phone call with Elaine, a thick packet arrived in the mail addressed to me in her tidy schoolteacher's script. Inside, I found a photograph of a group of people. I turned the photo over to read the inscription. "Here's my family and me at Christmas."

Brows knitted, I scanned the picture again, searching for her, the woman I had pictured as Natalie Wood for all those years, tall and willowy with straight dark hair and, possibly, a haunted look in her eyes.

That woman was not there.

Next I looked for someone who resembled myself, someone with my dark eyes, blondish hair, toothy smile. But the woman in the picture was a middle-aged woman with short, chestnut hair and big green eyes, wearing a striped shirt and navy blue pants.

As a thirty-three-year-old adopted woman looking at an image of my biological mother for the first time, I wanted to see my mirror image, as if it would reveal my identity. Elaine's photo offered no such clarity.

Still, I was fascinated. I had waited a long, long time to see images of people who shared my genetic material, real people with faces and feelings who lived in houses and drove cars.

They were no longer figments of my imagination. They were real, and that made me real too. I felt human, as if my Floating Space Baby self had been reeled back to Earth from her astral wandering by this picture of an ordinary woman who was not Natalie Wood, was no celebrity at all. She was the one who had sustained me in her body and birthed me onto terra firma.

I set the photos on the coffee table and walked to the drugstore to buy chestnut brown hair dye.

In our tiny bathroom, I tried to color my hair, staining several bath towels and most of my neck. But I did manage to dye it Elaine's color. I didn't tell Andy what I had done or why I had done it. I didn't tell anyone.

I knew it was a strange thing to do, but I needed to feel closer to Elaine. Now that I finally knew what she looked like, I craved connection with her more than ever. I wanted to make myself into a version of her. I had hoped for an immediate connection. Barring that, I at least wanted to look like Elaine or one of her kids. But that hadn't happened either. Now I had her hair color.

When Andy came home from the library, I waited to see if he would notice my new hair, but he said nothing about it. I showed him the photos of Elaine. He sat on the living room couch and squinted at the faces in her Christmas picture.

"Your eyes are similar to hers, I think." He was trying hard to be supportive. He knew how important it was to me to look like her. I had told him many times. "Maybe your cheeks, a little," he said, looking up at me. His eyes shifted to my hair. "Is your hair a different color?" he asked, leaning back to see it better.

"Yes."

I didn't tell him why I'd dyed it.

If other people noticed my new hair color, they didn't say anything. But every morning I looked at it in the mirror and tried to see Elaine in myself. And every afternoon, as I swam laps in the city pool, stroking through the water length by length, paddling toward nothing, I wondered why I didn't feel better, now that I knew who she was. I guessed my expectations had been too high. I wanted to become part of a clan who looked like me and thought like me. But I felt pretty much the same, drifting in the swimming pool day by day as the chlorinated water bleached my hair back to its sandy color.

A week or two after sending me that first photo, Elaine sent more: one of her as a baby riding in a stroller with a steering wheel; another as a preteen in a yellow Easter dress and prim white gloves; a third as a young woman graduating from college a few years after I was born; and finally, as a bride in her mid-twenties. Again I scrutinized them for similarities between us. We looked remarkably different, except in her graduation photo. She looked somewhat like I had when I graduated from college, decades later. Was it merely the look in our eyes, that anticipatory glint that people in their twenties have, or was it our long straight hair? Either way, it struck me that she looked the most like me around the same time she had made me.

Chapter 18

The Here and Now

(Davis, Chico, and Lake Tahoe, California)

her face broke and its smile appeared bending down towards me
saying there you are, there you are.

—Jorie Graham

Shifting my weight from foot to foot, I stood in my front hallway with them. Elaine, her husband Luke, and her daughter Tanya had just stepped out of my imagination and into our house. Elaine and I hugged, then took a step back and stared at one another. I couldn't help searching her face for a glimmer of resemblance. I had been hoping seeing her in person would reveal something I'd missed in the photos, but she looked exactly as she had in the first picture she sent.

Elaine broke the silence. "Look at you. Your pictures don't do you justice." She smiled, green eyes sparkling.

My face felt hot. Had she thought I was ugly in my photographs? I was hyperaware of her words, her facial expressions. All my senses were on high alert, taking in as much information as possible. I wanted to understand everything about her. But I was also hosting a dinner party for them. I had to remember that.

As if reading my mind, Andy offered to get everyone drinks.

Each grasping a wine glass, we walked to the backyard patio to sit. It was late summer, hot and dry, and everyone sweated a bit as they settled into our cheap plastic patio chairs. We watched Andy grill salmon fillets, chatting idly about their flight from Indiana, the conference in London that Andy and I had recently attended. I floated above myself in the conversation, participating but also watching myself participate. I wondered what I was getting myself into—who were these people?

For the rest of the evening, we all pretended what we were doing was normal, run-of-the-mill, as if having my birth mother, her husband, and her daughter over for a grilled salmon dinner thirty-four years after she relinquished me as a baby was no big deal. I marveled that this event was finally occurring and that no one, myself included, was commenting on the strangeness of it all. Everything felt airless and flat, a surreal parallel universe.

The next morning, we drove to Chico, my hometown ninety miles north, to introduce Elaine, Tanya, and Luke to my parents, who had recently reconciled and moved back in together. Days before Elaine arrived, I schemed with Andy to drive with Elaine in our two-seater truck so that I could get some time alone with her. I wanted to ask her questions I'd been too timid to ask over the phone.

At first, we discussed the landscape, the valley's dry heat so unlike the humidity she was accustomed to in Indiana. But twenty minutes into our journey, I couldn't hold back any longer. "What was it like in the maternity home?" I asked, voice squeaking.

She gazed out the truck's side window. "Oh, it was fine." Her tone was even and relaxed.

Fine? I screamed in my head. I pulled a can of Diet Coke from its cup holder, took a sip, and waited to see if she would say more.

"We each had chores we had to do," she said after a while. "I was in charge of the laundry." She continued looking out the window, the almond orchards flickering by. "There were a lot of girls there with me. We had a good time."

A good time? I choked on my Diet Coke. *Maybe she's trying to make light of it for my benefit. Maybe she's trying to protect me.* I began to understand I wouldn't get all of my answers during this visit. My stomach churned. She didn't seem to need to share her life with me. I wondered if we had differing visions of how we would fit into each other's lives—I wanted to know everything that had happened in the past to fill the blanks of my life from when she relinquished me until that moment in the truck. But she didn't want to go back in time.

Nothing more came of that conversation.

When we arrived in Chico, my mom answered the door, and she and Elaine hugged each other silently for a long time. My dad smiled and cleared his throat, then shook hands with Luke, and hugged Elaine and Tanya. Again, I felt like I was floating. We all walked out to the backyard, and Andy and Luke took pictures of everyone. Shaking with nervous energy and probably a little too much Diet Coke, I offered to get lunch ready, just to get away from everyone for a while.

In the kitchen, I gathered plates and silverware for lunch.

My mom walked in. "How are you doing, honey?" she asked, before grabbing napkins from a drawer.

"I'm okay, but this is really weird for me. What about you?"

"Oh, sweetie, I'm fine," she said, setting down the napkins and placing her hands on my shoulders. I looked down at the plates cradled in my arms. "I just hope this isn't too much for you. Elaine just told me the same thing out there." She glanced at the sliding glass doors to the backyard. I could see Luke, Andy, my dad, Tanya, and Elaine milling about in the garden, presumably making small talk. "We both know this is a really big moment for you," she said.

They were right. It was huge, and I had underestimated its impact. I looked up at my mom and tried to smile, but it was nervous, not genuine. Not wanting to talk about it anymore, I carried the plates and cutlery to the dining room.

After lunch, I suggested we go for a walk to the park, where every summer the city created a giant swimming pool by damming the creek. We ambled along the leafy sidewalks of my childhood neighborhood to get there. I still felt floaty. I wanted to get away again, submerge myself in the creek water—late on the eve of my wedding, I had furtively plunged into this same creek to calm my nerves.

I grabbed Andy's hand. "Let's go for a swim!"

Elaine laughed a little, as if she thought I was joking.

"She's practically a fish," my mom said. "You can't keep that girl out of the water." She smiled at Elaine. "Let's go sit while they swim," she said, gesturing at a park bench. The rest of them walked along the path in front of us.

"Isn't this a little rude?" Andy whispered, looking at me with raised eyebrows as he jogged with me toward the water.

"I have to get away for a minute. I'm freaking out. Everyone's acting as though this is normal, and it's not, and I don't know what I want from her. I don't know what she wants. I need to swim." I stopped and stripped down to my swimsuit.

He pulled off his shirt and tossed it on the grass. We jumped in and raced across the pool. He was much faster than me, but I didn't care. I needed an excuse to go as fast as I could, to outpace the silence of things gone unsaid for too long.

After our swim, everyone walked back to my parents' house for a belated celebration of Andy's and my one-year wedding anniversary. I could barely slice the cake my mom had ordered from a bakery.

Elaine noticed my unsteady hands at the cake. "You're shaking!" she said.

"I guess I'm kind of nervous," I said. I felt my jaw clench. I wanted her to know that meeting her was a strange experience for me, despite the veneer of calm and ease we were all working so hard to create.

We ate the lemon-raspberry cake, and everyone but me chatted.

I observed, unable to participate anymore. Luke, Andy, and my dad talked about college basketball. Elaine and Tanya sat with my mom, out of earshot. I watched, still feeling like I was having an out-of-body experience.

Just before we returned to Davis, I drove Elaine around town, showing her things I thought she might want to see: the cute downtown area with eclectic shops; the schools I'd attended; the tiny bungalow I'd lived in during my twenties. Last, I showed her the place I had run wild as a kid: the riparian park that ran through town, which had been the setting for Hollywood's version of *Robin Hood* in the early twentieth century.

Apart from my narration of the tour, there was mostly silence. Maybe Elaine didn't want to see all of it. Maybe it reminded her of the long-ago decision she had made to not share those kinds of things with me. Maybe she was as overwhelmed as I was by the visit and, like me, didn't know how to talk about it. There was no talk of how much adoption had hurt either of us: not the loss, the living apart, the not knowing, the wondering, the guilt, the shame, the grief, the secrets.

———————————

I had recently attended a conference about adoption, where I met Betty Jean Lifton, grandmother of adoption studies, psychologist, and author of books about the adoptee experience. She explained to me that it was a common experience for adoptees in reunion to want to go back in time to "the then and there, the moment of conception, the Navel of the World."

That was definitely what I wanted.

"But," she told me, "the birth mother doesn't want to go there. She wants to run away from it like it's a house on fire. She wants to be with her biological child in the here and now."

———————————

In the two-seater truck on the way back to Davis that evening, Elaine asked, "Do you think you got married so late because you felt at loose ends about being adopted?"

I didn't think I had gotten married "late," but I wanted her to know that adoption had upended my sense of self. I wanted her to know it had hurt me. I wanted it to hurt her, too. I didn't want to let her off the hook.

"Yes, I do," I said.

Silent, she looked out at the weather-beaten highway before us, then back over at me with a quick smile that was almost a grimace. Out of the corner of my eye, I could see that her eyes were wet.

———————

During the half-year after my first phone call with Elaine, Tanya and I had emailed each other a few times, and in one of her messages Tanya admitted she felt angry when Elaine told her about me all those years ago, realizing that my existence meant she was no longer the oldest child nor the only daughter in her family. She had been wary of how I might change her family's dynamics. Yet her curiosity about me seemed to override her anger and jealousy; she continued to email and phone me, inquiring about my relationships, my job, my writing.

For my part, I had grown up as an only daughter with two brothers, so I was excited to finally have a sister. But although we shared a mother, we were not exactly cut from the same cloth. We had some differences to overcome. I understood Tanya's wariness of me. And I was glad we shared an interest in each other. The day after we visited Chico, we geared up for a daytrip to Lake Tahoe, in the Sierra Nevada. Elaine and Luke would enjoy relaxing at the lake, and Tanya and I would trek a nearby mountain trail.

———————

It was a warm, clear day, and we loped up a dusty path, the yawning blue lake dropping off behind us. She asked me a thousand questions: What had I been like when I was in high school? What kind of music did I listen to now? Who were my friends now? What did we do for fun? How had I adopted my dog? Did I want to have children?

Before we met, I had relished thinking of Tanya as my doppelgänger, my alter ego, an analogue of myself in a different life. But the first thing I had noticed about her when she and her parents arrived at my house in Davis was that we didn't look anything alike. She had the graceful limbs of a long-distance runner, and she was tall, with gray-blue eyes and dark brown hair. Very unlike my short, solid frame, my green-brown eyes, my blondish hair. And the more we talked, hiking along, the more differences we identified: our political leanings were diametrically opposed; our views on religion did not overlap. Musical taste? Completely divergent. Performing karaoke? One thumb up, one down. The list of incongruities stacked up like the domes of igneous rock we hiked across at the crest of the range. Still, we were drawn to each other, so we kept trying to unearth common ground.

We did both like hiking, so on and up we trekked, over the crest and down its far side and back again, beginning to find our footing with each other.

The next day, the three of them came over to our house for breakfast before packing up to go to the airport for their return trip to Indiana. As we munched bagels on my backyard patio, anxiety flared in my stomach: the visit had felt like a dream, an airy soap bubble breathed into shape by hope that would pop and disappear once the sun shone on it. I was afraid that when Elaine left, I would never see her again.

I tamped down my anxiety enough to say, "Andy and I are going to visit his parents in Chicago for Christmas. I was wondering if we might drive down to Indiana to see you, too."

Elaine's eyes lit up. "That would be great." she said. I was surprised at her enthusiasm, given her relative aloofness throughout the rest of her visit. "Tanya and Matt will be home for Christmas," she added, "so you'll be able to see them as well. To have all of you together would be wonderful." She hadn't called me her child, but she had implied it, kind of, so maybe she did want to think of me as family.

"It's a plan then," I said, voice bright. I eyed Andy, hoping the idea was okay with him. He gave me a tiny nod and smile. The bubble would remain intact a while longer.

We finished breakfast and rose from the table. I still could not fathom saying good-bye to Elaine, even though I now had a plan in place to see her in a few months' time. A leaden feeling weighted my body, primal and sorrowful. Andy and I walked them to the door and hugged them good-bye. Hugging Elaine last, I laid my head on her shoulder and rested it there for a moment, eyes closed. *Don't let her leave you again,* the leaden feeling warned. *Do not let her out of your sight.*

Our hug ended. "See you at Christmas!" Elaine said, tears in her eyes.

My heart raced. I thought I might throw up.

The three of them walked to their car to drive to their hotel to pack. I watched from the front porch, unable to move.

As the car disappeared around a corner, Andy squeezed my shoulders. "I think the visit went well, don't you?" he asked.

I could barely hear him. The leaden primal something had taken over my ears, my head. I was in another world. I nodded, still looking out across our shaggy front lawn toward the corner they'd just rounded.

"Sweetie," Andy said gently. "Now that they're gone, I really need to get back to work on my dissertation. Are you okay? Do you want to go for a swim?"

I looked up at him. I did not want to go for a swim. "I'll be fine," I said. "I think I'll ride my bike to the farmers' market, get some fresh air." I still felt like I might throw up.

"Sounds good." He squeezed me again before heading back into our house.

I reached inside the front door and grabbed my keys, unlocked my bike from the front porch's wooden railing.

The farmers' market was only a few blocks away. I pedaled as fast as I could, trying to leave behind the heavy feeling. I parked my bike and walked through the throng of Saturday morning shoppers carrying coffee cups and baskets of produce. I stared at ample mounds of late summer tomatoes, the season's final peaches, the hopeful early harvest of almonds. I couldn't stomach the abundance.

I retrieved my bike and again pedaled fast, counting the blocks to their hotel, hoping I would find them there. I pulled into the parking lot, where I saw them wheeling their suitcases toward the rental car.

Hoping I didn't look as crazed as I felt, I dismounted my bike and walked toward them, trying to relax my muscles. "Hi!" I called, waving. The dreadful sensation in my abdomen ebbed slightly; Elaine still existed, she had not disappeared into the ether.

Luke looked up from the trunk. "Andrea! What are you doing here?"

Elaine walked up. "Hello, stranger," she said. She laughed, then cocked her head to one side. "Did we leave something at your house?"

I tried to think of a good reason for my presence in the hotel parking lot. "I was just on my way from the farmers' market and saw you walking to your car." I took a quick breath. "And I wanted to say good-bye one more time."

"Oh, honey," Elaine said, reaching over to give me a hug. "It was great to meet you. And we'll see you again in a few months."

I held her tightly for a few moments, my breathing slowing. Then I hugged Tanya and Luke again too.

"Do you want help loading your car?" I asked, not ready to leave.

"No thanks, I think I've got it," said Luke, smiling and waving me off. I wondered if he thought I was crazy.

I stood in the parking lot, watching them pack the trunk, and waved good-bye when they drove off. The gruesome feeling of loss had dulled.

Chapter 19

Half Sister

(Davis, California)

i could no more ignore
the totems of my tribe
than i could close my eyes
against the light flaring
behind what has been called
the world

—Lucille Clifton

Tanya and I kept in touch after her visit, frequently emailing each other and talking on the phone. She was one of the first people I told when I became happily pregnant.

She told me about her misgivings about her engagement to her long-term boyfriend. I sent her pictures of my growing belly. She emailed me that she'd finally decided to break off her engagement. I called her when my son, Owen, was born, sent her videos of him learning to crawl.

When he was one year old, and a very active toddler, I was home with him almost full time and longed for some adult company. On the phone, Tanya told me she was moving out of her apartment and was thinking of living with her parents for the summer while she planned a move to southern California.

"If you want to live in California," I said, "why don't you come out here and live with us for the summer? I'd love to see you." Making that offer seemed like the big-sisterly thing to do, but I doubted she would accept—we had spent a sum total of three days together, and she was very close with her parents, who were expecting her to move in with them.

———————

She took me up on my offer. On a July afternoon, she arrived at the Sacramento airport towing a huge red suitcase and moved into our converted-garage spare room.

She was courteous and helpful, and she loved baby Owen. She ably took care of him while I went to my part-time job teaching creative writing classes at a nature preserve. And he loved her.

Tanya became quite popular among all my new-parent friends and their babies. She went with us everywhere: to birthday parties for one-year-olds, dinner parties, even mind-numbing trips to Costco for huge boxes of cheap diapers. And to the beach—I took her surfing with some friends in the chilly water near Bolinas. Afterward, she and I hiked along a coastal bluff to a lake in Point Reyes National Seashore, taking turns pushing Owen in his jogging stroller up hills and over rocks. It felt like we were really sisters.

Most important to me were the hot summer evenings she and I spent in the rickety wicker chairs on my front porch. After I put Owen to bed, Tanya and I talked and laughed, drinking white wine. We continued creating our common ground, learning about each other, leaning into familiar places and being curious about the unfamiliar. We persisted with each other, each refusing to give up on the other. It was important to both of us that we were biologically related: sisters who met as adults, sisters who grew up in very different families, but sisters nonetheless.

Near the end of summer, Tanya landed a great job in San Diego. I was sad she would be leaving. I had loved her companionship. Loved her.

———————

She fell in love with a man in San Diego and eventually got engaged to him. She and I often talked on the phone during the months she planned their wedding. I liked hearing the latest details—the cut of her dress, her choice of shoes, a new idea for the perfect venue.

One day, she was telling me about flowers she'd ordered. "There will be little wreaths around candles on each table during dinner. Purple and blue."

"Nice!" I said, keeping an eye on Owen as he ran his wooden trains along their tracks.

"I'd like you to be in the wedding," she said. I gasped. "And I was hoping you could read a poem during the ceremony." It felt like a step forward in our relationship, a new point plotted on the map we were making.

"I'd be honored," I said, breathless, thinking, *Did she really just ask me to read a poem in front of everyone she knows and loves?*

At her wedding, I sat in the audience waiting for my turn to approach the altar and read a poem I'd composed for the occasion. Andy stood at the back of the crowd, in charge of our wiggly three-year-old. Jiggling my leg, I thumbed through the program and saw I was listed as "Sister of the Bride." My heart jumped—seeing it in print made it more real than before, a public declaration by Tanya and Elaine that they had claimed me. I was no longer a secret nor a source of shame or sorrow. I sat sweating under the heavy Indiana sun, exulted and terrified.

Two ladies seated near me whispered to each other as they read the program. "Sister of the Bride?" one said, pointing at a page, then looked up at her friend, brows furrowed.

"That bride doesn't have a sister!" the other answered, then flapped the program like a fan.

She does now, I thought.

But my confidence soon cracked. *After half a lifetime spent apart from them*, I wondered, *could I truly gain a sister, a mother?*

Who determines the paths blazed through landscapes? What cartographer maps the topographic lines of inchoate relationships fissured by loss and reshaped by reunion?

At the microphone in front of the altar, I drew myself up to my full five feet four inches. The hollow feeling of not belonging gnawed at my stomach as wind gusted, but I took a deep breath and attempted to read my poem without feeling like the bastard child crashing the party.

The previous night, after the rehearsal dinner, Andy had taken Owen to our hotel room to put him to bed, and I stayed at the bar to chat with my half brother Matt and his friends. I had spent very little time with Matt and wanted to get to know him better.

Matt and I were chatting when one of his friends approached. "So, how do you two know each other?" the friend said.

Matt and I looked at each other for a long moment. A small smile spread on my face and I looked down. I didn't want to be the first to speak. I wanted him to take the lead, to let him tell his friend whatever he saw fit. I was curious what he would say.

Matt laughed a little, raised his beer bottle and took a long pull. "We're related. . . . She's my half sister."

"Ha!" Matt's friend said, clapping Matt on the back. "Good one."

"My mom had a baby when she was a teenager," Matt said. He took another pull of his beer.

Silence.

"That's me!" I said, shifting my weight. I smiled goofily and slung my arm around Matt. Then I looked up at him, eyebrows raised.

He gave me a quick smile.

His friend stared at us, still speechless.

"I'll let Matt fill you in on the details," I said. Setting my beer on the table, I waved good-bye.

As I walked down the hall toward my hotel room, I heard Matt's friend say "Seriously, are you shitting me? I thought she was your old babysitter or something."

Before the ceremony that afternoon, Elaine had called Andy, Owen, and me to a gazebo on the hotel grounds for the family wedding photographs. "I definitely want one with all three of my kids," she told the photographer. "And my grandson!"

We all posed on the gazebo steps, smiling for the camera, together, like a family. I thought of a letter Elaine had once sent me:

Dear Andrea:

This is the second anniversary of the night that Shirley called
me to ask if I was interested in reconnecting with you, one of
my happiest days. Since I got a second chance to have you in my
life, I have tried to be a citizen of a "kinder, gentler" world—I
figure the least I can do is pass my second chance on to others.

I've never told you that I love you, but I do—and I need to start
telling you."

She loved me. I loved her. And I was grateful to have her in my life.

What I didn't have with Elaine was a shared past. I wasn't sure there
was any way to make up for thirty-odd years of not knowing her. I couldn't
help recalling what she had told me about some of her friends who were
adopting a baby. They told Elaine the birth mother was twenty-one years
old, attended nursing school, and had lots of younger siblings—so she
knew how hard it would be to get through school while mothering a baby.

"They're all getting what they want," Elaine told me. "Everyone is going to be happy."

Not everyone, I thought, stomach tightening.

"I have a special place in my heart for that birth mother," she said,
acknowledging the very thing I had been thinking: that she knew the pain
of being the woman who left the hospital without a baby. Her candor surprised me. Perhaps she was beginning to trust me enough to make herself
a little vulnerable to me. Maybe I could do the same with her.

It seemed a dam had begun to breach—jagged concrete chunks of it
breaking free and rolling downstream, eroding into tiny particles, becoming sand, and forming new beaches in a canyon. Sure, rough edges would
remain, resistant to the smoothing effects of water and time. But the river's renewed flow would slice through old sediment, churning and ex-
huming long-buried objects: eyeglasses lost in an upset in Hermit Rapid,
early explorers' skeletons, fragments of John Wesley Powell's boat, plastic
water sandals, mining tools, raven wings, elk antlers, shriveled blue juniper berries, lost loves. The bedrock would be scraped clean. Everything
would move after decades of stillness.

Chapter 20

Effects of the Edge

(Philadelphia, Pennsylvania and Northern Colorado)

where wounds will bathe, bedded in sand,
one edge rushing over to enfold the other.

—Sandra McPherson

There was one person I hadn't found yet in my search for my biological origins. Elaine had written his name, Theo, and address on a scrap of yellow paper and included it in one of her letters. I pinned it on my office bulletin board, where it remained for years, until Andy got a new job in Philadelphia, and he, Owen, and I prepared to move across the country. Packing up my office, I slid the little slip of paper into my wallet, and there it stayed as we transitioned into our new life far from California. We moved to Philadelphia without knowing a single soul.

I had never lived farther east than New Mexico, but now I found myself in a leafy Philadelphia neighborhood, in a big, fixer-upper of a hundred-year-old house. Andy worked long hours at his new job, so I had plenty of time to trawl the local playgrounds with Owen, trying to make friends. We met some other young families, but I felt out of place in that unfamiliar landscape, and so far from family. Perhaps it was why I finally considered contacting my birth father, Theo.

I dug up several photographs of Owen and me and had them enlarged, hoping that humongous pictures of a long-lost daughter and an adorable grandson would make it impossible to ignore us, would make us real enough to merit a response. I wrote a letter explaining who I was, sent it with the photos by registered mail, and prepared to wait.

I received a call right away. The first thing Theo told me was that as soon as he read the letter, he picked up the phone to call me. The next thing he told me was that he hadn't known I existed until he read my letter. My heart pounded—Elaine told me Theo knew, had driven her to the doctor to get the pregnancy test that confirmed my presence all those years ago. Was Theo denying knowledge of Elaine's pregnancy? Or was he surprised that the pregnancy had resulted in a child—me—being born?

It must have been chilling to receive my letter. I hadn't written the kind of letter one might write to a person who doesn't even know one exists; I had written it assuming he knew he had a long-lost child wandering around in the world somewhere.

———————

"I thought I had four kids," he said, sounding jovial, "but now I have five. I'm happy to have you as a daughter!" I liked hearing that, but I tried to keep my expectations in check—I had no idea who he was.

I told him about my Ankylosing Spondylitis.

"I'm sorry to hear that," he said, sounding surprised and saddened. "I hope it didn't come from my side, but I can't think of anyone in my family who had anything like that."

My chest tightened. Why I had developed a chronic illness remained a mystery.

He told me about himself, that he liked to camp and fish, lived on the same tract of land on which he had grown up on Colorado's Front Range. Like me, he preferred wide open spaces to forests and cities. I nodded, even though he couldn't see me. His last revelation made me wonder if we are all somehow hardwired to love our ancestral landscapes.

———————

A month later, Theo sent me an invitation to his wedding. I had already been the bastard child at one wedding. Could I do it again? When Tanya got married, I had been developing relationships with her and Elaine for years. I had never even met Theo, nor his bride, kids, mother, or anyone else who would be at the wedding. I thought attending the wedding would be a great way to meet everyone all at once. But I couldn't face the idea of being the forgotten daughter who crawled out of the woodwork at his nuptials. I declined his offer, feeling sad and relieved.

We phoned each other intermittently and exchanged birthday and Christmas cards, me always dodging the question of when we would meet each other. When he shared the news that his mother, my grandmother, had died a few months after his wedding, I felt the sting of missing the chance to meet her. I decided I needed to meet him before someone else was lost forever. I finally got brave enough to suggest I travel to Colorado to meet him.

In *Twice Born: Memoirs of An Adopted Daughter,* Betty Jean Lifton chronicles her life as an adopted person, including her search for and reunion with her birth parents. She recounts her school-aged son approaching her with a homework assignment to create a family tree, asking her to help him draw her side of the tree. "Does the adopted person go on the tree she was placed on biologically," she wonders, "or the tree onto which she was transplanted?"

The time had arrived to explain to my six-year-old son the intricacies of what Lifton called her "family arboretum," her alternative to a family tree.

Several weeks before boarding the plane to Colorado, I told Owen "We're going on vacation to see Theo!" as we ate dinner.

"Who's Theo?" he said, struggling to cut a piece of chicken with his butter knife.

I took a deep breath, preparing to tell him that Mommy has two fathers; one is Grandpa Bob, whom she grew up with, and the other is Theo, whom we would visit in a few weeks.

But before I could get a word out, Owen swallowed his last bite of chicken, set down his knife, and said, "Can I have dessert?" He had moved on, without so much as a tug on the branches of my personal arboretum.

At first, I took Owen's response as a sign that he wasn't ready, it wasn't the right time. But my reluctance to spell it all out was about me: I was afraid when he learned I have two dads and two moms, he would wonder who was the "real" dad, the "real" mom. I knew he would ask why I hadn't grown up with the parents to whom I was born, and I worried he would wonder if he, too, would be given to another set of parents. I cringed at the thought that he might ask, "Why did your parents give you away?" because I still wondered that myself sometimes. Even though my rational mind knew that at eighteen my birth mother could not have kept me, could not have parented me alone, didn't have support from her family, had been shamed by society for getting pregnant outside of marriage, the part of me I called the Floating Space Baby still didn't understand. I didn't want Owen to know about that part of me. I thought it would scare him—it scared me.

Owen and I were snuggled up on the living room couch one morning, him in footie pajamas as I read aloud *The Magic School Bus: Inside the Human Body*.

He patted my belly. "Mommy, was this my home before I was born?"

"It was."

He unzipped his pajamas and pointed to his navel. "And you fed me through here?"

"Sure did." I wiped sleep out of my eyes. It had been an early wake-up kind of morning.

"I didn't have a mouth, so I needed to eat through my belly button."

I ruffled his blond curls. "You did have a mouth," I said, "but you ate through your belly button."

"What happened when salad tried to go through there? Did it get stuck?" He laughed. "Or tomatoes? I hate tomatoes, so when a tomato went through there I spat it right out. But mashed potatoes would fit. They would just slide right through!"

I took a sip of tea. "I guess so," I said. It was awfully early in the morning for anatomy and physiology.

"I love you, Mommy." He curled up closer to me.

"I love you, too." I hugged him tightly, then released his chubby little body. I felt very lucky to have carried him in my body, to have given birth to him, and to be able to have that conversation with him. I didn't know why he was obsessed with his belly button, but I knew why I was. I loved knowing that we had once been connected by a cord, that he would never have to feel like a Floating Space Baby.

But I was a little nervous about what other people would think when he started telling them that he spat tomatoes out of his navel.

"Mommy, did I kick you when I lived inside your belly?" he asked.

"Yes," I said. "Like this!" I tickled his belly.

He shrieked and squirmed out of reach. "What did you say when I kicked you?"

He loved to ask me this. "I always said, 'Baby! What are you doing in there?!'" I looked down at my stomach and made a funny face. He laughed, and I went back to reading to him.

He wasn't finished. "Mommy, did you kick Grandma Sharon when you lived inside her belly?"

My throat tightened. But I thought of the strength of the redwoods, the live oaks, cedars and redbuds, all the trees I loved, and breathed in, calling on them to help me explain my family arboretum to Owen.

"No . . . I didn't live there."

He sat up. "What?"

"I lived inside Grandma Elaine's belly instead," I said, then held my breath.

"You did?" he said, eyes wide.

"Yes, and when I came out, Grandma Elaine decided I should live with Grandma Sharon and Grandpa Bob."

"Why?" he asked. The million-dollar question. It always stopped me cold.

I punted. "Because Grandma Elaine decided it would be a good idea if I lived with Grandma Sharon and Grandpa Bob."

"Oh," he said, picking up a toy school bus he had parked under a throw pillow. He rolled it across my belly. End of story. I had told him I was adopted, only not in so many words.

A week before we left for Colorado, seven live caterpillars, black with brown stripes, arrived in our mailbox. A birthday gift for Owen. The caterpillars lived in a clear plastic container. For days, they ate, grew, and crept around their little capsule, spinning thready webs upon which they inched their way across its slick walls. Soon they began to migrate to the container's lid, where they fastened themselves by their tail ends, curling like inverted fiddleheads. Then they bloated and turned into chrysalides, letting what looked like their heads fall off in the process. Furry caterpillar noggins rolled on the container's floor. When tiny spikes appeared on the chrysalides, iridescent orange and yellow, Andy and Owen transferred them to a mesh butterfly container.

Outside my window, a thunderstorm clamored, sky broken into shards of dark clouds and sunlight. I gazed out the window and watched a hummingbird trying to land on the spidery pink blossoms of my neighbor's mimosa tree. I was bedridden. After one more day, I would be allowed to leave my bed and resume my life. A few short days after that, Andy, Owen, and I would board a plane bound for Denver to meet Theo.

I had hung the butterfly cage in my bedroom so I could watch them as I was confined to bed after my embryo transfer, the last stage of in-vitro fertilization. I imagined the little embryo attaching to my uterine wall, the way the caterpillars had webbed themselves to the lid of their container. I pictured the microscopic bundle of DNA implanting, growing, and changing like the chrysalides that twitched when I gently jostled their cage. I did it every so often, to confirm that there was something alive inside.

This was my last chance. Andy and I had been trying to conceive a second child for three years, including one previous IVF attempt, to no avail. We had exhausted our meager savings, so this was our last stop on the fertility train.

When I was allowed out of bed, the outlines of wings were visible inside the chrysalides. I reentered my life as the mother of a young child, trying to envision myself pregnant, once again growing a full moon of a belly, becoming the mother of the little person who could come of all that medical spell-casting. When I focused inward, though, all I could see was darkness. I heard nothing.

———————

All seven of the chrysalides split open, and a painted lady butterfly, orange with black and white dotted wingtips, emerged from each. Owen and I plucked purple coneflowers from our yard and dipped them in sugar-water to feed the butterflies, who alighted on the wet petals, unraveling their long proboscises to drink. They stayed in their mesh cage for a few days, and the day before we left for Colorado, we released them into our sunny urban yard.

Owen and I watched them as they flitted about the garden.

"I hope they decide they want to live here," he said.

I pulled him close. "I bet they'll love the flowers in our yard."

But they flew over the hedges and out into the city—flitters of smoky sunshine, transplanting themselves from our home to somewhere beyond.

Watching the butterflies fly away, I thought about how adopted people are transplanted too—from one family to another, which made me think of what I had learned while working in the Grand Canyon: Aldo Leopold's observation that species living at the juncture of two life zones, called the ecotone, adapt to both environments. Perhaps then, adoptees also dwell in a kind of ecotone. Could we be what biologists call edge species? If so, what could that mean?

———————

We landed at Denver International the next night, and I called Theo to tell him we'd arrived. He said he'd invited a bunch of family members to gather at his house the next afternoon for a backyard cookout in honor of our visit. My heart pounded upon hearing this news. I still wasn't sure I could handle a big group.

While Owen and I waited for Andy to get a rental car, we made a game of spinning in circles in the windy darkness outside the airport while looking up at stars we never got to see in light-polluted Philadelphia. The spinning addled my head as much as what we were about to do spun my emotions. I would not only meet my biological father for the first time, but I would also meet my half brothers, nephews, uncles, and who knew who else? I had butterflies, maybe painted ladies, in my stomach.

––––––––––––––

Deciding to meet Theo was paired inextricably in my mind with that final attempt to get pregnant: both were about the need to know. I needed to know my biological father. And although I had been beaten down by my experiences with infertility, I needed to try overcoming it one final time. Our previous IVF attempt had been stressful, and I had hesitated to go through the hoping against hope all over again, but I knew that if I didn't try, I would always wonder if that final bid would have been the one that worked. After all, those caterpillars had hatched into butterflies against the odds, hadn't they?

––––––––––––––

On our way to Theo's the next day, we drove into Longmont, Elaine's hometown, and parked in front of an address she'd given me. The house in which she grew up was white clapboard, its windows shuttered against the summer heat, and it had one of those merry-go-round-style clothes-lines in the side yard behind a low fence. Nobody answered when I knocked on the door. I half expected a white-haired lady wearing a floral house dress to emerge and shoo us away with a pillowcase. I lurked around a bit, looking at everything, waiting for ghosts to appear. I crept around to the back of the house through the alley, peeked between fence slats into the backyard, hoping no one would call the cops.

I imagined Elaine, an only child, playing on the sunny lawn, perhaps sitting in that stroller with a steering wheel I'd seen in the baby pictures she sent, waiting on the concrete patio to be taken for a jaunt, honking its fake car horn. Maybe digging in the sandbox in the corner of the yard, patting clumps into elaborate castles. Or picking and eating cherry tomatoes on the sly from a garden patch. Maybe in the deep night, sneaking out the gate near the spiderwebbed garage to meet her boyfriend, my birth father.

The only ghosts who appeared there were the ones I imagined.

Theo lived outside the next town. We drove through its dusty streets, up onto bluffs where paved roads turned to packed dirt. Surrounded by pastureland atop a plateau, we found the county road he lived on, and, after a mile or so, turned up a driveway.

A stout, balding man wearing a Hawaiian-print shirt stood next to a farmhouse, scanning the road.

"That's him," I said quietly, trying to catch a better look as we parked. As he waved us down, I noticed smiling eyes behind his wire-rimmed glasses. "Here we go." I glanced at Andy quickly, tried to control my panic. I hopped out of the car, leaving him to unbuckle Owen from his booster seat.

"Theo?" I said. I recognized his face from one of the few photographs he'd sent me.

"Hello, Andrea!" he exclaimed with a big smile, and he wrapped his arms around me in a hug. My eyes teared up, and I was glad that he had come out to meet us alone, away from the party, and what sounded like throngs of relatives gathered in his backyard. Eventually, our hug dissolved, and we both reached up to wipe our eyes.

"Nice to meet you," I said, unable to think of anything less ridiculous.

Owen and Andy drew near. Theo introduced himself to my family while I scrutinized him, looking for similarities. *Eyes, maybe,* I thought. *I go all squinty when I smile, too.* I remembered something Theo said when we first spoke on the phone.

"In your pictures, you look just like one of the family."

He led us into the backyard and began introductions. There were about twenty people there, all related to me. It was the first time I'd been in a big group of blood relatives. First I met my brothers: Nick was tall, stocky, and a computer whiz, and Nolan was a deeply tanned general contractor.

Nolan's two young sons were blond, like Owen. Delighted to have more cousins, Owen ran off with them to learn how to drive a golf cart around Theo's pasture.

Next I met Theo's uncle, who was visiting from southern California and had decided to extend his stay to meet me. I met Theo's new wife and Theo's brother and sister-in-law. They walked us down the road to their farm to bottle feed twin Jersey calves whose mother couldn't produce enough milk.

While we were feeding the calves, Theo grilled up a huge slab of beef ribs for everyone, and when we returned, an afternoon thunderstorm swept in, drenching the patio furniture. We all scurried to an enclosed porch to eat. In that small space, Andy took photograph after photograph: me with my new, burly, adult brothers; Theo and me sitting next to each other on the porch with dazed smiles on our faces; Owen playing with Theo's antique toy tractors.

Like the thunderstorm that interrupted the party, I felt I had swept in and knocked things out of place. Again. It was exhausting. We said good-bye and made plans to go hiking with just Theo the next day.

———————

He drove us to a trailhead at a large reservoir. Andy slowed to Owen's pace so Theo and I could hike together. As we circled the water, Theo pointed out his favorite flowers and the birds flitting in the bushes, something I, too, love to do when hiking. Our paces fell in step with one another.

———————

Later, when I looked at photos Andy took, I found one of Theo and me snapped from behind as we walked along the reservoir, our strides in lockstep with one another. That was what I had longed for: to fall into rhythm with my origins. To find someone I could relate to about the little things I have done all my life that seemed to have no identifiable agent.

———————

Lanky grasses dried by the long summer brushed against our legs as we walked, and Theo reiterated something he'd told me the first time we spoke on the phone: "I'd rather be outside than anywhere else."

"I've always felt the same way." I breathed a quiet sigh. There is an intimacy in the simple rhythms created by walking with another person. It has cemented many of my closest relationships: Andy and I took long hikes on some of our first dates and on many subsequent ones. Throughout my life, I have created family by walking with others, setting down the beats of a life lived together.

We rounded a bend that opened into a flowery meadow, where small greenish-white butterflies rose, surrounding us. I hoped it was a sign I was pregnant, that the fertility treatments had worked against all odds, that everything was coming together. I had found Theo; perhaps I would be blessed with another baby, my family would be complete, and I could finally be whole.

But then I saw they were moths, not butterflies. They flapped away a moment after we spied them, and I felt emptiness in my body. I knew I wasn't pregnant.

The next day we said good-bye to Theo and drove higher into the Rocky Mountains to hike some more. Even though clouds threatened a thunderstorm, Andy, Owen, and I strode through an alpine meadow full of electric-colored wildflowers—orange paintbrush, purple lupine, yellow asters. I waved them ahead and sat down a log. Although I risked getting caught in the rain, I needed to be alone. I had visited a clinic that morning for a pregnancy test and had learned I was not pregnant. I wanted so badly to have another child, but now I had to come to grips that it was not to be. I hadn't even told Andy yet.

I sat numbly in the chill air, watching a nearby creek, its tiny rapids moving over fist-sized stones, swirling the green rafts of summer leaves downstream. I stood and hurled rocks into it and cried.

Finding my way back to the trail, I heard splashing from a thicket of aspen trees upstream. The sky cleared, and the air became hot and close. As I rounded a bend, I saw Andy and Owen in a clearing with a deep pool. Again they splashed, drenching each other with creek water. I slipped behind a tree. Palming its bark, I craned around it to watch them in the hard sunlight as they played together and shrieked with joy.

This was my family. I was starting to accept that Theo and his sons were my family too. As were Elaine and Tanya and Matt. And of course, my mom and dad and brothers were my family. My life was thick with edge effect, my biome overlapping with all of theirs in ways I was only beginning to understand.

Chapter 21

Front Range

(Philadelphia, Pennsylvania and Northern Colorado)

So take the lovely air,
And, lovely, learn by going where to go.

—Theodore Roethke

T heo and I kept in touch, talking on the phone from time to time. One summer morning, he called. My half brother Nick had died. Suicide. He was forty-five.

Nick was a smart and witty and troubled man. When I met him at the party in Theo's backyard a year earlier, we had joked that since we were born only three months apart, but to different mothers, we were long-lost twins. Only it wasn't really a joke. The fact that he was born to his mother just a few months before I was born to Elaine had launched us in divergent directions like a malfunctioning slingshot. The fact of his birth had shaped his life and mine. I often wondered what my life would have been like if Elaine had gotten pregnant before Nick's mother did, if Theo had married Elaine instead. I had even envied Nick.

———

"I'm so sorry, Theo." I paused, not knowing what else to say. "Thank you for telling me."

"I know you and Nick kept in touch." His voice cracked into a sob. "I wanted to make sure you knew right away."

I offered consoling words and thanked him again, said good-bye. I rubbed my forehead, wondering if I should attend Nick's memorial service. I had only met him once, but we had kept in touch via telephone and email. Would Theo want me to be there? I wanted to support Theo and honor Nick, but did I belong at the funeral? I felt an ache in my throat. If your brother dies, you go. This was trickier. Was Nick my brother? Yes and no. Once again, I was in the position of not wanting to be an outsider at an intimate family event, a person whose presence people would question or judge.

I asked my friend Abby, an adoptive mother, for advice. "This is a decision of the heart," she said. "If you feel moved to be there to express your sadness and sympathy, then go. You belong."

I decided if Theo wanted me there, I would go.

I parked myself on the living room couch and called him.

"How are you doing?" I asked, knowing it was an awful question, but unable to think of anything better.

"I have good moments and bad," he said, voice shaking a little. "I never thought I would have to plan my own child's funeral. It's not supposed to happen this way."

"No, it's not. It's a terrible thing," I said, my own voice cracking. I took a breath, let it go. "I'm wondering if you think it would be okay if I attended Nick's memorial."

I heard him choke back a sob. His pain was palpable. "That would be great," he managed to say.

"I'll be there. I'll call you when I've made flight reservations," I said before breaking into tears myself. Andy heard me and walked in from the kitchen, sat next to me on the couch, his arm around me.

"I'll talk to you soon, Theo," I whispered, unable to speak normally.

"Talk to you soon. I love you," he said.

"I love you too." I hung up. Andy sat with his arm around me while my body shook.

I cried hard. It didn't matter if I was a "real" daughter or sister. Nick was gone, Theo was hurting, and I was a person who cared about both of them. Boundaries that I'd drawn around "family" and "not family" blurred as the muggy Philadelphia air slunk in through my living room window and engulfed me. Surrounded by the many overlapping feelings about all the people in the widening circle I called family, I didn't have to be tough anymore or prove I was a badass just to feel that I was like someone or unlike someone else. I could just be a person in relationship with others who cared about me.

Nick knew the effects of the edge all too well. He lived in the liminal space between mental illness and health. Did the circumstances of his own birth, his parents' shotgun wedding, their early divorce, influence his well-being? I certainly wondered the same about my early circumstances—whether the trauma of being taken from my birth mother as an infant made me vulnerable to the chronic disease my body manifested when I was a teenager.

Whatever the case, Nick and I both grew up on the edges of families, each of us straddling the threshold between one and the other, and between states of health and disease.

Biologists tell us that edges of life zones are rich in diversity—and sometimes more dangerous for their residents. But what if, instead of viewing my edges as places of tension, conflict, or jeopardy, I could see them as stepping-stones I could use to hop from one to the next? What would I find? Could I create a continuous procession of zones, with permeable, all-encompassing edges?

Perhaps those wounded, vulnerable places could become, as Rumi wrote, the "Places where the Light enters."

After Nick's memorial, I took a walk on the gravel road in front of Theo's house. I wasn't alone: Nick's fluffy Australian shepherd, Sparky, followed me through the gate and insisted upon trotting alongside me, even when Theo called him back.

I had an impulse to call Elaine, to tell her the tragic news about Nick, to draw everyone together at last, as if I had the wind's expansive arms and could collect people like scattered leaves. Elaine hadn't seen Theo since before I was born, when he married Nick's pregnant mother. Now, Theo knew the unparalleled pain of losing a child, like Elaine did. Perhaps that would afford them common ground. We were all heartbroken, but we might heal, and we might help each other to do it.

The road's small stones crunched beneath my sandals as if settling into place. Sparky's claws ticked rhythmically, echoing my footsteps. Together we walked, paralleling the Front Range, that unlikely juncture between the Rocky Mountains and the Great Plains.

My gaze swept along the panoramic landscape, and for a moment I could see the ragged edge of each landform converging in the rippling summer heat.

Afterword

Wilderness delivered me from one family to another and back again, providing me a home as I traveled between the known and the unknown. During the decade I searched for my birth parents, the wild outdoors became my family. But affinity with the land is not unique to me. In ancient Greek, *omphalos* means "navel." It also refers to a sacred stone the oracle of Delphi rested upon that afforded her direct communication with the gods. Called the Navel of the Earth, the omphalos was a place of connection and knowing.

Indeed, many world cultures honor sacred stones as stand-ins for navels, using them to represent humans' connection with the Earth. For example, the Hopi people of the southwestern U.S. esteem the Sipapu, or Place of Emergence, which connects them to their ancient ancestors. Spanning cultures and millennia, these navels illustrate the intrinsic human need for connection both with forebears and with the Earth; they allow us to understand ourselves in relation to those who came before us and connect us to that which is larger than ourselves.

Such understanding is impossible if we don't know where we came from. Concealing people's origins not only deprives them of their biological identity, but also disconnects them from the larger human family. The emphasis on secrecy in closed adoption detaches adopted people from their biology and breeds shame. Open adoption, which affords adopted people some degree of connection to their families of origin, helps quell feelings of abandonment and displacement but unfortunately is not a perfect solution. In many open adoptions, birth or adoptive parents choose to terminate contact with the adopted person. This happens for a variety of reasons, not the least of which is that maintaining contact can be emotionally painful. My greatest hope for dispelling the secrecy and shame adoption evokes is the normalization of all types of families.

Knowing our origins helps us to forge connections with our larger human family. The world is in the midst of a crisis of identity: the trend is toward splitting off into individuated, self-defined units. Knowing and reflecting on our origins is perhaps our most powerful way of resisting this trend as it compels us to locate our families, including the biological family that connects us to all others. In a larger sense, reflecting on our origins inevitably leads us to the metaphorical navel, that which connects us to the source from which we all derive, the Earth.

Acknowledgments

D eep gratitude to Betty Jean Lifton and Nancy Verrier, grandmothers of adoption writing, for paving the way for this book. To Sharon and Bob, my mom and dad who raised me, and my brothers Brian and Jason with whom I grew up, thank you for enduring the machinations of my search. Even when it was difficult to understand why I needed to do what I was doing, you supported me. Carol, Francis, Erin, Michael, Tye, and Trevor, thank you for your grace, and for allowing me to barge into your lives and ask uncomfortable questions. I can't imagine *not* knowing you.

Early readers of this book and support sisters extraordinaire, Wordspace superheroes Eileen Flanagan, Ellie Stanford, Hilary Beard, Jude Ray, Lori Tharps, Meredith Broussard, Miriam Peskowitz, and Tamar Chansky get my heartfelt thanks. I couldn't have asked for a better writers' group. Thanks also to Naomi Williams, Rob Faus, Linda Turpin, Amy Whitcomb, Julie Ackerman, Jane Carroll, Susan Chambers, Julie Odell, Nicola Waldron, Sue Morgan, and Jason Ross for revision insight and encouragement. John Aubert, thanks very much for the science consultation.

Voluminous gratitude and giant love go to my mentors Lucille Clifton, Sandy McPherson, Gary Snyder, Alan Williamson, and Al Young: you helped my writing self bloom.

Many thanks to the folks at CavanKerry: to Joan Cusack Handler and Gabriel Cleveland for believing in this book and guiding it into being. To editor Baron Wormser for improving it, and copyeditor Joy Arbor for her careful attention to every word and idea—I am bowled over by your dedication. You made the book so much better. And to marketing whiz Dimitri Reyes for shouting it to the world.

This book was fostered by the generous gift of time at the Mesa Refuge. A scholarship to the Bread Loaf Environmental Writers' Conference came along at just the right moment.

Kim Nalder, thanks for letting me talk your ear off about this book every time we went backpacking in the desert. David and Jeannette Robertson, much gratitude and love to you for your listening ears while I navigated the publication process. Robin Holm and Amy Youngs, thanks for putting up with me in the frontcountry and backcountry ever since we were three; lifelong friends like you are rare treasures.

Abby Ruder, adoption specialist and all-around wise woman, you have helped so many people touched by adoption, including me. Thank you for your listening ear, affirmation, and guidance as I wrote this book. You are my hero.

Owen, my first and only, thank you for making me a mother and for letting me write about you, you wonderful, inspiring person. I couldn't love you more.

Andy, you are the one who stayed, and boy, am I lucky.

Source Acknowledgments

I would like to thank the editors of the following journals, anthologies, websites, and a podcast, in which parts of this book, in earlier versions or with alternative titles, have previously appeared:

Connected: What Remains as We All Change (Wising Up Press):
    "Half-Sister"
The Dirtbag Diaries Podcast: "Double Vision"
Permanent Vacation, Volume 2 (Bona Fide Books): "Ask a Ranger!"
The Ploughshares Blog: "Effects of the Edge"
Portrait of an Adoption: "Empty Boots," "Ruins and Ladders"
Raising Mothers: "Slapped"

The author and publisher gratefully acknowledge the following:

The book epigraph is from "Lost in Translation" by James Merrill in *Collected Poems*, published by Knopf.

Chapter 1's epigraph is from "Meditation at Lagunitas" by Robert Hass in *Praise*, published by The Ecco Press.

Chapter 2's epigraph is from Flannery O'Connor's September 6, 1955 letter to Betty Hester, published online in *The American Reader*.

Chapter 3's epigraph is from "I'm Nobody! Who are you?" by Emily Dickinson in *The Complete Poems of Emily Dickinson*, published by Harvard University Press.

Chapter 4's epigraph is from "Make a Law So the Spine Remembers Wings" by Larry Levis in *The Darkening Trapeze: Last Poems*, published by Graywolf Press. Copyright © 2016 by the Estate of Larry Levis. Reprinted by permission of Graywolf Press.

Chapter 5's epigraph is from "The Colors of Darkness" by Chana Bloch in *Swimming in the Rain: New and Selected Poems 1985–2015*, published by Autumn House Press.

Chapter 6's epigraph is from "Coal" by Audre Lorde in *The Collected Poems of Audre Lorde*, published by W. W. Norton.

Chapter 7's epigraph is from "Climbing" by Amy Lowell in *A Dome of Many-Coloured Glass*, published by Houghton Mifflin.

Chapter 8's epigraph is from "Snapshots of a Daughter-in-Law" by Adrienne Rich in *Collected Poems: 1950-2012*, published by W. W. Norton.

Chapter 9's epigraph is from "The Rescued Year" by William Stafford in *Poetry*, July 1964.

Chapter 10's epigraph is from *Slaughterhouse-Five* by Kurt Vonnegut, published by Modern Library.

Chapter 10 includes "i am accused of tending to the past" by Lucille Clifton from *The Collected Poems of Lucille Clifton*, published by BOA Editions. Copyright © 1991 by Lucille Clifton. Reprinted by permission of BOA Editions.

Chapter 11's epigraph is by Patti Smith from *All Songs Considered* Guest D.J. Patti Smith, June 19, 2012.

Chapter 12's epigraph is from "My Shoes" by Charles Simic from *Charles Simic: Selected Early Poems*, published by George Braziller, Inc.

Chapter 13's epigraph is from *The Faerie Queene* by Edmund Spenser.

Chapter 14's epigraph is from "The Delicacy" by Sandra McPherson in *Patron Happiness*, published by The Ecco Press. Copyright © 1983 by Sandra McPherson. Reprinted by permission of the author.

Chapter 15's epigraph is from "After the Shipwreck" by Alicia Ostriker in *Poetry*, July 1979.

Chapter 16's epigraph is from "Riprap" by Gary Snyder. Copyright © 1958, 1959, 1965 by Gary Snyder, from *Riprap and Cold Mountain Poems*. Reprinted by permission of Counterpoint Press.

Chapter 17's epigraph is from "Photographs" from *Miniatures and Other Poems* © 2003 by Barbara Guest. Published by Wesleyan University Press and reprinted with permission.

Chapter 18's epigraph is from "Cagnes Sur Mer 1950" by Jorie Graham in *The New Yorker*, March 14, 2011.

Chapter 19's epigraph is from "hands" by Lucille Clifton in *The Collected Poems of Lucille Clifton*, published by BOA Editions. Copyright © 1991 by Lucille Clifton. Reprinted by permission of BOA Editions.

Chapter 20's epigraph is from "Edge Effect" by Sandra McPherson in *Poetry*, July 1995. Reprinted with permission of the author.

Chapter 21's epigraph is from "The Waking" by Theodore Roethke in *Collected Poems of Theodore Roethke*, published by Doubleday.

Recommended Reading

Brodzinsky, David, Marshall D. Schechter, and Robin Marantz Henig. *Being Adopted: The Lifelong Search for Self.* New York: Anchor Books, 1993.

Eldridge, Sherrie. *Twenty Things Adopted Kids Wish Their Adoptive Parents Knew.* New York: Dell Publishing, 1999.

Fessler, Ann. *The Girls Who Went Away: The Hidden History of Women Who Surrendered Children for Adoption in the Years Before Roe v. Wade.* New York: Penguin Press, 2007.

Glaser, Gabrielle. *American Baby: A Mother, a Child, and the Shadow History of Adoption.* New York: Viking, 2021.

Lifton, Betty Jean. *Journey of the Adopted Self: A Quest for Wholeness.* New York: Basic Books, 1994.

—*Lost and Found: The Adoption Experience,* 3rd ed. Ann Arbor: University of Michigan Press, 2009.

—*Twice Born: Memoirs of an Adopted Daughter.* New York: St. Martin's Press, 1998.

May, Gerald G. *The Wisdom of Wilderness: Experiencing the Healing Power of Nature.* New York: HarperCollins, 2007.

Pavao, Joyce Maguire. *The Family of Adoption: Completely Revised and Updated.* Boston: Beacon Press, 2015.

Verrier, Nancy Newton. *The Primal Wound: Understanding the Adopted Child.* Baltimore: Gateway, 2012.

—*Coming Home to Self: The Adopted Child Grows Up.* Baltimore: Gateway, 2003.

CavanKerry's Mission

A not-for-profit literary press serving art and community, CavanKerry is committed to expanding the reach of poetry and other fine literature to a general readership by publishing works that explore the emotional and psychological landscapes of everyday life, and to bringing that art to the underserved where they live, work, and receive services.

Other Books
in the Memoir Series

Unnatural Selection was typeset in Arno Pro, which was created by Robert Slimbach at Adobe. The name refers to the river that runs through Florence, Italy.

This book was printed on paper from responsible sources.